"As a CEO, you may be bombarded with a never-ended barrage of ideas to improve your effectiveness. With everything you learn and implement, there seems to be another around the corner. In *Made to Thrive*, Brad Giles compresses years of hands-on experience and study, coaching CEOs to be more effective, into a concise manual that you can follow step-by step. Not only does he outline what to do, he links it to what really matters for your company: your firm's performance."

—KAIHAN KRIPPENDORFF

Founder, Outthinker and author of *Outthink the Competition*, *Hide A Dagger Behind A Smile* and *Way Of Innovation*

NEW YORK, NEW YORK

"Growing a business to be more purposeful, meaningful and useful in the world is a big goal for many of us CEOs. But, how do you do it? Well, one of the answers is that you'll need to grow your own knowledge, skill and understanding of how to be an effective CEO first. Brad Giles' model to help us CEOs assess our skills and then take action to move from good to great is the practical and powerful guide I wish I had much earlier in my career."

—TRISTAN WHITE

CEO and Founder, The Physio Co and author "Culture is Everything"

MELBOURNE, AUSTRALIA

"As a CEO it's often lonely at the top. *Made to Thrive* provides a clear blueprint on how to be a great CEO and how to make a bigger difference in a world full of disruption. Brad is a highly talented and experienced executive coach. His coaching together with the 5 roles outlined in *Made to Thrive* have helped Aventus scale up significantly and given me a blueprint on how to be a great CEO. "

—DARREN HOLLAND

CEO, Aventus group

SYDNEY, AUSTRALIA

"As a CEO of 20+ years and now as a Coach to High Growth CEOs world-wide – this book is a must read for every CEO. Brad has done an excellent job in laying out clear and immediate action steps to realize a GREAT return on all your efforts as a CEO. This CEO playbook will ensure you are providing maximum results for your business."

—SHANNON BYRNE SUSKO
Serial Entrepreneur, Strategic Execution Expert,
and Best-Selling Author *The Metronome Effect* and *3 HAG WAY*
VANCOUVER, BRITISH COLUMBIA

"*Made to Thrive* is a very powerful resource for CEOs looking to become more effective."

—TIM CLARKSON
Managing Director, Chas Clarkson
SYDNEY, AUSTRALIA

"Brad's extensive knowledge and ability to get to the root of issues has yielded wonderful results."

—DARREN KAM
Managing Director, Constructive Media
PERTH, AUSTRALIA

"*Made to Thrive* nails the key requirements for effective leadership in business. This book makes a perfect reference for those wanting to create great companies. It distils some of the best research in this area and applies it sensibly and practically. The simplicity of language, and, direct approach, makes it ideal for everyone to read, re-read and refer to often. The tools offer real examples of how to apply the principles of leadership as a CEO. As a CEO myself, I will use this book regularly and ensure I cover all aspects of each of *Made to Thrive*. I am impressed with this book and recommend it highly."

—STEVE STANLEY
Director, WA CEO Institute
PERTH, AUSTRALIA

"For all enlightened and dedicated CEOs looking to not just grow a great company, but also develop themselves as an inspiring and effective leader, *Made to Thrive* is a must read. Brad Giles' five part framework and accompanying exercises, as well as his compelling stories, help you evaluate your strengths and your weaknesses as a CEO. Then, he gives you the tools to put in place an action plan to leverage your talents and grow yourself – as well as your organization."

—CHERYL BETH KUCHLER
Founder and President, CEO Think Tank®
PHILADELPHIA, PENNSYLVANIA

"I found *Made to Thrive* confronting in terms of what I am not doing, exciting because of the possibilities it opens up, and honest because it does not beat around the bush. But above all, practical because it confidently and succinctly establishes the rationale for actions and provides tools to do them."

—RAGHAV MEHRA
CEO, Denver Technology
PERTH, AUSTRALIA

"If you're looking to take your impact as a leader to a higher level then *Made to Thrive* is a step-by-step handbook explaining how to do just that. Brad is an insightful and thought provoking coach who will make you look at things from a different perspective, and challenge you to greatness."

—HAZEL JACKSON
CEO, Biz Group
DUBAI, UNITED ARAB EMIRATES

"Brad has been working with our leadership team in developing our strategic plan. Brad is precise, quickly sees past a smoke screen and helps us be real about what is required to make change to improve. He has been able to challenge our ideals, keep us accountable for our promises and bring a clearer strategic direction that will set the business foundations for many years to come."

—TONY POOLE
CEO, Parasyn
BRISBANE, AUSTRALIA

"Brad is a battle-tested field general of entrepreneurship and business coaching who has redefined the path to success for busy CEOs with a step-by-step practitioners guide on how and why to redefine your role as a leader, and ultimately what success means to you."

—TOBI LAWRENCE-WARD
Managing Director, Abaxa
PERTH, AUSTRALIA

"I have the privilege of working with Brad who leads the development of our strategic plan and the facilitation of our annual and quarterly workshops. Since we've been working with Brad we have seen a great shift in the way we operate our business. Brad has shared a wealth of knowledge with our executive team and helped us prioritise our goals and become disciplined in achieving them."

—CARLY COHEN
Director, Maple Event Group
MELBOURNE, AUSTRALIA

"Having been in communication with Brad throughout his journey of authorship and a significant time as a Premium Business Coach; and then experiencing his work on *Made to Thrive*, I am both impressed and delighted for the clarity, practicality and actionability of what he has created in content, story and tools for CEOs."

—KEITH CUPP
Founder and CEO, Gravitas Impact Premium Coaches
PORTLAND, OREGON

"Brad has been working with our team in developing our strategic plan and facilitating strategic workshops for many years. Brad has challenged us, kept us accountable and brought a clearer strategic direction that has set the business foundations for years to come. *Made to Thrive* is an excellent resource for any leader and the concepts can be applied to any business, at any time for near immediate results!"

—DAMIAN COLLINS

Managing Director, Momentum Wealth and President REIWA

PERTH, AUSTRALIA

"*Made to Thrive* is a simple and powerful resource for any leader that is written in a manner which both respects the reader and provides a direct path to action and real results!"

—KEVIN LAWRENCE

Founder, Lawrence & Company Growth Advisors Inc.
and author "Your Oxygen Mask First"

VANCOUVER, BRITISH COLUMBIA

"*Made to Thrive* is a simple and effective practitioners guide on how to create a greater impact, and where to focus as a leader."

—ADAM TAYLOR

Managing Director, TCD group of companies

PERTH, AUSTRALIA

"*Made to Thrive* provides a clear roadmap to extraordinary performance for those who lead or aspire to lead high growth firms. Brad Giles has produced a practical, actionable framework for CEOs to improve their effectiveness and accelerate profitable, sustainable growth."

—MARK E. GREEN

Speaker, Strategic Advisor, Coach and Author of *Activators: A CEO's Guide to Clearer Thinking and Getting Things Done*

WARREN, NEW JERSEY

"Brad's work with the Geographe team and myself has been hugely valuable over the years and *Made to Thrive* is a great progression on the work we've done, providing a high level, no-nonsense look at what to focus on, and in what order. Then when you think you're done? Take the assessment and go again for that higher level!"

—SAM HYDER
CEO, Geographe Enterprises
PERTH, AUSTRALIA

Made to Thrive

MADE TO THRIVE

*The Five Roles to
Evolve Beyond Your
Leadership Comfort Zone*

BRAD GILES

BOOK DESIGN: Kevin Barrett Kane at *The Frontispiece*

To my children Amelie, Cameron,
Reece and Mitchell, and my wife, Maggie.
Thank you.
You make me Thrive.

CONTENTS

★ START HERE

How to be effective. That's every leader's problem.

The question you are asking yourself, either consciously or unconsciously, is, *"How can I make my potential count for the most in this world of effort?"*

And this is absolutely the question you should be asking.

But not in order to achieve fame for the sake of fame, nor to acquire money for the sake of money, but for the sake of usefulness in the world. For the sake of helping those you love. For the sake of benefitting society.

I am writing to those who work and strive, for I have given up on those who have given up. Whether you are the president of a kid's football club, the leader of a not for profit, a business owner, the CEO of a billion dollar corporation, or anyone in between, this book is for you.

I want to help you become more effective and make your potential count for more.

This book began with a simple question.

What is the difference between a good CEO and a great CEO?

In this world of endless meetings, emails and new management fads, how can a CEO, the final decision maker, exchange his or her effort for the greatest results to scale a business with happy customers, shareholders and employees as well as healthy financial results?

These questions sat with me for more than a decade as I worked with some of the best CEOs and CEO coaches from around the world, trying to understand both what great CEOs do different, and what tangible impact those differences create.

The more I shared this question with CEOs and leadership teams, the more I realised that many CEOs are often uncertain what to do in their role in order to produce the maximum impact on their company. I couldn't find a book defining *how* to be a great CEO. Many books analyse the attributes of a successful company, but none seemed to approach what a CEO themselves should and should *not* do in their role.

With this book I have focused on filling that absence by creating a definitive practitioners handbook outlining what a CEO must do in his or her executive role, in order to create great results.

Without knowing what roles they must fulfil to reach those great results, many CEOs end up doing 'OPJ', Other People's Jobs, such as 'helping' the sales manager or 'helping' the COO. This distraction not only removes accountability from the person being helped, it prevents the CEO from doing his or her important roles.

There's rarely a prescriptive job description on *how* to be a great CEO. Furthermore, there's little consequence when a CEO produces only good results instead of great results because they, or the major shareholders, or the board are often willing to accept "good" results. For example, a board might accept a 5% profit result with a 5% revenue growth. They might not love it, but they might accept it. The main question then is could that CEO be more effective if he or she focused on his or her role and avoided doing other people's jobs? If they were in fact doing other people's jobs and not performing their role would there be a consequence? Without consequences for producing good results, which of course means lesser results, a CEO won't know what they are missing. They'll end up simply filling in the gaps.

Perhaps the biggest problem with this negative feedback loop: when no one holds the CEO accountable for producing good instead of great results, the CEO finds very few opportunities to learn and grow.

As Jim Collins succinctly described it, 'Good is the enemy of Great'.

Five results

In the 2017 Harvard Business Review article, "Why do we undervalue competent management?", authors Raffaella Sadun, Nicholas Bloom, and John Van Reenen from Harvard Business School, Stanford University, and MIT respectively, describe their ongoing research project with the Centre for Economic Performance at the London School of Economics. The project, commenced in 2002 and still running, analysed 12,000 companies across 34 countries to determine the impact that key management practices have on the results of a company.

And this observed impact, throughout this enormous project is indeed profound. The article details that moving a firm from the worst 10% to the best 10% of management practices is associated with the following results:

★ Attracting more talented employees
★ Fostering better worker well-being
★ 75% higher productivity
★ 25% faster annual growth
★ $15 million increase in profits
★ Spending 10 times as much on R&D
★ Increase in patenting by a factor of 10

Therefore, as the CEO is leading the management team in any organization, the team that ultimately manages all activities, these are the type of measures that should be used to determine the efficacy of the CEOs effort. For the role of a CEO broadly is to ensure that the management team are producing the best results by utilizing the best and most appropriate management practices.

In other words, according to the research these are broadly the metrics by which great results from a CEO are defined.

It has been my interpretation and observation, which correlates with these research findings, in working as an entrepreneur, manager and leadership coach over the past 20 years that there are five main results that great CEOs produce, in comparison to the results of average or good CEOs. These five results are:

★ **HIGHER PERCENTAGE OF TOP PERFORMERS** - top performers, the top 10% within an industry, are attracted to working for great CEOs who are producing better results. These highly motivated and driven employees simply *can't* work for leaders they don't view as being great. They might tolerate a good CEO, but only until they can find a better leader to join. They know a CEO who isn't great is impacting their career, and they are acutely aware that they want their potential to count for the most.

★ **HIGHER RETENTION** - great CEOs are good role models and positively impact culture, causing employee engagement and satisfaction scores to rise. Subsequently, employees tend to stay longer as great CEOs provide less reason to leave.

★ **HIGHER PRODUCTIVITY** - great CEOs get a higher return for each dollar paid to employees. People in the organisation are more effective because both a successful strategy generally produces a higher gross profit relative to their compensation and an attractive culture is conducive to a more productive environment.

★ **CONSISTENT GROWTH** - you can bank on a great CEO growing the business every quarter and every year. The efficacy of strategy, its ability to drive revenues and profits, and its ability to actively consider all potential growth-affecting issues, ensures that growth occurs no matter the environment.

★ **CONSISTENT RESULTS** - there are no surprises with great CEOs. They have successfully mitigated risks and have built a group of employees and suppliers who do what they're supposed to do when they're supposed to do it, achieving the goals they set and producing the expected results quarter after quarter.

Five roles

Each of these results occur as a direct result of the leader implementing and executing particular management practices within the business and performing certain practices him or herself. It is these practices, or roles, that a CEO must undertake in order to achieve these great results that forms the premise of this book.

While there are many changes that can impact these results, there are five key roles that should be performed by the CEO that will have the greatest effect on these great results. Let's briefly define the five roles now.

★ **ACCOUNTABILITY** - There is accountability for all employees and suppliers. A great CEO makes sure people completely understand what is expected of them. Results are transparent and consequences are clear.

★ **AMBASSADOR** - The CEO performs a strategic role as an ambassador. Great CEOs know you can't be the head of the company without being the face as well. They are involved in the engagement process for employees, customers, plans and initiatives.

★ **CULTURE** - A positive culture unites the team and attracts the right people. By consciously building a great culture that delivers on the needs of the right people, great CEOs become magnets for great talent.

★ **STRATEGY** - The company's strategy delivers a unique and valuable position in the marketplace that is different than its competitors. Great CEOs rely on a strategic system. They focus on becoming and remaining different within their industry.

★ **SUCCESSION PLANNING** - Key risks to the business are reduced through succession planning. Great CEOs build systems to insure against people, products, customers or investments failing to perform. They are deliberately protecting the consistency of staff and supplier output and revenue stream consistency, knowing the impact on growth and profit.

Consider each of these roles as displayed in the star to the right. Each point of the star is a different role, requiring different effort in a different direction.

This book is structured around these five roles. The goal is to look at these roles and help a CEO create a better return on his or her effort. Each of the five chapters in this book represent one of the five roles outlined above.

Within each of these five roles, there are five habits to establish and maintain in order to dramatically impact the results you produce as a CEO. With that in mind, each of the five chapters in this book are divided into five sections. So there are twenty five sections with each section containing a principle, a story and a tool to help you implement the habit into your business.

Each of the twenty-five sections contained in the five chapters is represented in the checklist below. So as soon as you have completed

ACCOUNTABILITY

SUCCESSION PLANNING

AMBASSADOR

STRATEGY

CULTURE

the checklist below you can see how many of these sections may be useful to you.

This book is designed to be simple, practical and actionable. I want it to be useful for you.

With this aim, I want you to write all over the pages, fill out the forms, complete the tools, make notes on what you're thinking everywhere. You can download copies of the tools at my website, evolutionpartners.com.au, but remember that these pages are designed to be used and marked up.

So grab a pen and begin by completing the checklist below to see how your current habits and roles compare to the habits and roles we'll be covering in the book.

Made to Thrive checklist

1. There is accountability for all employees and suppliers
- ❏ All employees understand every aspect of what it takes to succeed in their role
- ❏ All employees report to their peers weekly on the two key performance indicators (KPIs) which define their role
- ❏ Failure has a consequence that is transparent and is known by all employees and suppliers
- ❏ All team meetings are conducted with an agenda, and data is available to effectively make decisions during meetings
- ❏ Internal and external employees and suppliers who do not consistently perform are rapidly removed from the business

2. The CEO performs a strategic role as an ambassador
- ❏ The CEO has a system to build a public profile, such as industry forums, industry leadership, blogging or speaking
- ❏ The CEO attends all major customer contract signings or product launches
- ❏ All employees learn Core Values and Core Purpose stories monthly from the CEO
- ❏ All new employees are welcomed by the CEO either physically or virtually within their first week of employment
- ❏ Every quarter the CEO launches the company plan and priorities to all employees

3. A positive culture unites the team and attracts the right people
- ❏ Core Values and Core Purpose are known by all employees
- ❏ There is a qualitative and quantitative system of feedback between all employees and leaders
- ❏ Ideal Employee needs are identified, and the Employee Promise helps to attract the best employees at the pay you offer

❏ Employee Promise KPIs are measured weekly, and performance is displayed all around the business

❏ Where Core Values breaches occur, employees are reprimanded or terminated

4. The company's strategy delivers a unique and valuable position in the marketplace that is different to competitors'

❏ Quarterly and annually, the leadership team meets off-site to reflect, evolve the company strategy and set priorities

❏ The company's long term 10+ year BHAG® is known by all staff, and actions are taken each quarter to progress toward the BHAG®

❏ Ideal Customer needs are identified, and the Brand Promise is helping to attract the best customers in the market

❏ Brand Promise KPIs are measured weekly, and performance is displayed all around the business

❏ Each key product or service contributes to the company hedgehog. Any which do not are discontinued

5. Key risks to the business are reduced through succession planning

❏ Each significant role within the organisation has a virtual bench of at least two people who are contacted quarterly

❏ Products and services at risk of decline or disruption are mapped quarterly, and actions identified to replace these revenues

❏ Suppliers at risk of decline or disruption are mapped quarterly and actions identified to replace these suppliers

❏ All decisions on new opportunities, new staff or new investments are evaluated against a documented set of criteria

❏ Each leader in the business has appointed a clear successor who could replace them from within

This checklist is designed to identify opportunities for you to improve. Through the years, as I've worked with CEOs using this checklist, some have only marked one or two boxes from 25, and others have checked 18. That's okay. This isn't a competition. This is about you, exploring your opportunities to improve and chase great results, and helping you become more effective.

Next, using the star to the right, color in the corresponding check boxes that relate to each of the five roles. For example, if you checked three of the accountability boxes in the checklist above, color in three of the checkboxes in the accountability line below. Go through and complete this for all five roles. Ultimately you'll come away with an easy-to-read, visual representation of what roles are strongest in your company, and what roles could use strengthening.

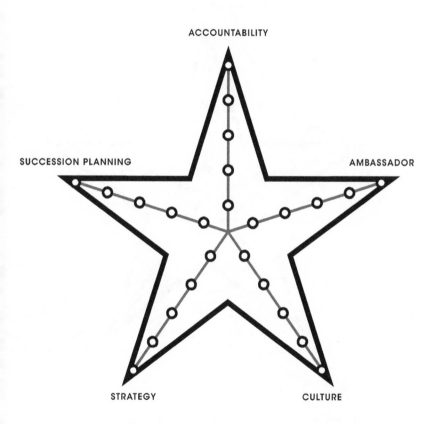

Now draw a line between the last boxes you marked on each role line. By doing this, we'll create a radar chart on your star that looks similar to the example one below.

What you have now identified is your ranking against the *Made to Thrive* checklist. The star graphic we started with has become what's called a radar chart. You can see the things you are doing currently compared to the things you are not. Maybe you're hitting three of the successful company habits around the Accountability and Culture roles, but only one habit around Succession Planning (as shown above). It's easy to see where you need to focus your work.

Let's recall the five results mentioned earlier that great CEOs create

★ Higher percentage of top performers
★ Higher retention
★ Higher productivity
★ Consistent growth
★ Consistent results

Each one of the five results outlined above are dependent on the roles the CEO is executing on. For example, the first result of a great CEO, having a higher percentage of top performers, occurs because the CEO has executed on the Accountability role *and* the Ambassador role. If the CEO performed an outstanding job as an ambassador yet there was little to no accountability, there would be a lower percentage of top performing staff because top performing staff thrive in a high accountability environment.

If the CEO had a fantastic strategy that created strong top line growth, that growth would be jeopardized if suppliers or staff or products were not available to execute on that growth, if there wasn't a reliable succession plan in place to maintain the consistent execution.

The combination of these two roles and their interdependency create the output which is the relative result between the roles in the star.

From here, we can assess how each of the results are related to each of the five roles.

Successfully completing both the Accountability role and the Ambassador role will create the HIGHER PERCENTAGE OF TOP PERFORMERS result.

Successfully completing both the Ambassador role and the Culture role will create a HIGHER RETENTION result.

Successfully completing both the Culture role and the Strategy role will create a HIGHER PRODUCTIVITY result.

Successfully completing both the Strategy role and the Succession Planning role will create the CONSISTENT GROWTH result.

Successfully completing both the Succession Planning and the Accountability role will create the CONSISTENT RESULTS result.

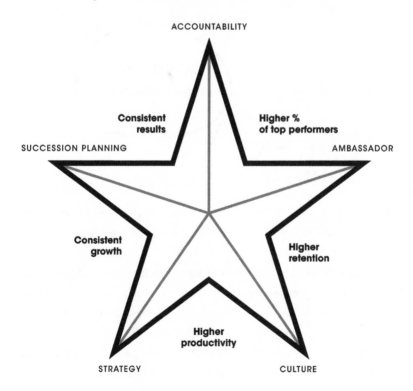

So go back to your radar chart and look over the areas where you scored high and scored low. Can you see a lower score correlated with lower results in your business?

For example, if you scored lowest on Culture and Ambassador, are you having problems with employee turnover and retention? I would love to hear your personal business stories as well, so please take the time to e-mail me your results at brad.giles@evolutionpartners.com.au and please share photos of your *Made to Thrive* radar chart on social media with the hashtag #madetothrive.

Getting outside your comfort zone

Have you seen the internet meme below about your comfort zone?

It beautifully illustrates how the magic happens outside one's comfort zone and how to achieve real results one must step outside their comfort zone.

Let's now overlay that onto the sample radar chart in the diagram below. The line you have drawn around your checkboxes on each point outlines your comfort zone. These are the things you are comfortable doing. This principle applies across all five results.

However, if you want to transition from being a good CEO to being a great CEO, you must step outside your comfort zone.

Practically, this means scoring 3 or higher in both roles that affect a result. The more space your radar chart occupies outside the star, the more you will achieve the results in that area.

As you can see below, if you scored 3 on both Accountability and Ambassador, you will be slightly outside the star, and slightly out where the magic happens, scoring a 5 on both will place you where the higher percentage of top performers result is most likely.

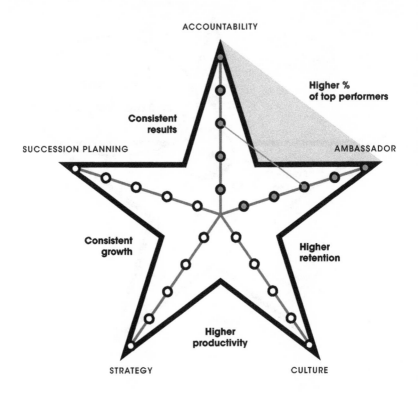

ACCOUNTABILITY

Higher %
of top performers

Consistent
results

SUCCESSION PLANNING

AMBASSADOR

Consistent
growth

Higher
retention

Higher
productivity

STRATEGY

CULTURE

Let's take a look at an example broken out in detail.

Steve is our CEO. He runs a technology company. Steve scored 1/5 on Accountability, 3/5 on Ambassador, 3/5 on Culture, 5/5 on Strategy and 4/5 on Succession Planning. Steve has good growth and productivity, but his results are inconsistent, with fluctuating revenues and profits, furthermore, not everyone on his team are top performers. In fact, there are several people he wouldn't enthusiastically rehire.

Steve's opportunity is to work on the accountability role with the desired objective to create more consistent results and a higher percentage of top performers. He should focus on the four accountability habits he hasn't checked off. In chapter one, using the tools related to each un-checked accountability habit, he should be able to develop a plan to strengthen his approach to accountability as the CEO.

In order to push out to where the magic happens and generate consistent results and a higher percentage of top performers, Steve needs to evaluate his role in accountability and improve those results.

Look at the radar chart below. In it, we see that Steve has a clear plan to improve each of these two results he originally struggled with.

★ HOW TO USE THIS BOOK

First, don't get overwhelmed by the amount of work to do and don't feel your score is anything but an awesome opportunity. You are probably already a really good leader. But I've written this book to give you tools that can make you a truly great leader.

Second, appreciate that you can't do everything at once. Understand that there is only one of the twenty-five tools in this book that you should implement first, and that first one should be the one that creates the most impact for you and your business. Then the second, then the third, and so on. Your first job is to prioritize the tools in this manner.

This book is a tool, a resource for you, and it's meant to be used in the way that best fits your needs. This is a collection of best practices; it's up to you to determine how to best make these best practices work best in your business.

The leaders I know and have the privilege to work with are some of the hardest working and most dedicated people one could find, and I'm proud to know them, but no one I have met dreams about building a mediocre or a good business, people dream about building a great business.

Aiming for greatness is never easy, but don't short change yourself. This is your legacy, your life's work. Make it great.

Key points

- ★ There is a fundamental difference in the results that great leaders produce when compared to good leaders
- ★ This difference, when compared against different research studies repeatedly produces results in similar areas
- ★ I have also observed this difference in my experience as an entrepreneur and a business coach
- ★ The five main results that demonstrate the distinction are
  - ❏ Higher percentage of top performers
  - ❏ Higher retention
  - ❏ Higher productivity
  - ❏ Consistent growth
  - ❏ Consistent results
- ★ It is my postulation that these five results are predominantly produced by five main roles that a leader undertakes being
  - ❏ Accountability
  - ❏ Ambassador
  - ❏ Culture
  - ❏ Strategy
  - ❏ Succession planning
- ★ Without clarity on what roles to do, many leaders perform other people's jobs and neglect their own important roles
- ★ The manner in which these roles impact the results is outlined in the remainder of this book

Key Resources

- ★ "Why do we undervalue competent management?" Harvard Business Review September 2017 - Raffaella Sadun, Nicholas Bloom, and John Van Reenen

★ ACCOUNTABILITY

1.0 There is accountability for all employees and suppliers

In the seminal 1974 Harvard Business Review article by William Oncken Jr. entitled, *Who's got the monkey?*, a manager grapples with his workload while his subordinates identify problems supposedly shared between them that require a 'next move.' They continually give these problems, which Oncken calls 'monkeys,' to him making him far too busy to complete both his work and work on their problems.

One Saturday morning while driving to the office to solve the problems given to him by his four subordinates, the manager notices that they are in fact playing golf together at the local golf course. He then realises who is working for whom and how his good intentions to help his staff with problems has in fact meant that his team are not taking responsibility for their roles.

This article has been one of the most successful HBR articles ever and has created the popular phrase 'Get the monkey off your back'.

After almost 45 years this article is still powerful enough that I have every one of my clients read it at some point, and every time it has a significant impact on how they view their role, and how unconsciously from the very first day they have structured their relationship with staff to make them avoid responsibility. At the very beginning they find themselves telling staff 'if you have a problem, don't hesitate to come and ask for help'. It seems innocuous enough, but it develops a habit that prevents staff from solving problems by themselves. Once this habit is sufficiently developed, the independent, problem solving part of their brain seems to quickly shut down.

While this failure to have team members independently solve problems can have a crippling effect on efficiency and effectiveness, there is a second equally damaging habit that can be fostered in teams without a strong discipline of individual accountability. Social psychologists call it 'social loafing'.

Way back in the 1890s, the psychologist Max Ringelmann proved that the more people there were in a group, the less work they did.

Imagine your team was in a tug of war contest pulling a rope and your competitors were at the other end of the rope. In one example a single person is in a tug of war against a single person who works for your competitor. However, in the second example, your whole team of eight is pitched in a tug of war match against the competitors team of eight. You might think that the average force exerted by team members would be the same in both examples. Ringelmann proved that between one and eight people, the force exerted per person reduces between five and ten percent each time you add a person to the team. That's around half the effort in a team of eight.

FORCE EXERTED VS. NUMBER OF PEOPLE IN THE GROUP

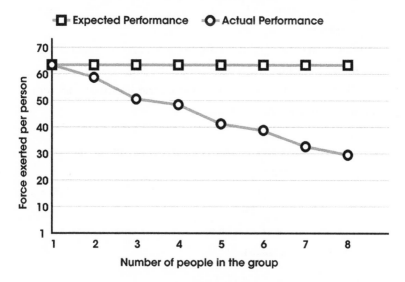

But it is not just limited to humans: loafing is prevalent in the animal kingdom also. According to a scholarly article in the International Society for Behavioural Ecology, scientists from the University of Minnesota have proven that the ideal wolf pack size is four and that every wolf over a pack of four is simply a freeloader only there for the kill.

Imagine if you were asked to sing happy birthday by yourself at a party. Then instead, what if you and seven of your friends were singing it together? The group provides the ability to seek camouflage behind the efforts of your fellow singers.

Across a wide-ranging set of tasks, psychologists have further validated Ringelmann's findings that in a team measured by the overall output, rather than individual output, the average effort exerted is significantly lower.

Once you have people who are accountable and solving problems, you have two of the three key ingredients to achieve overall higher accountability. There is no point measuring people individually if there isn't a consequence when they consistently fail to produce the agreed-upon results.

When managing staff, these are three major problems I suggest a large number of CEOs and leaders suffer. The simple ways to overcome these three problems, which have such a significant impact on the productivity of team members, are to:

★ Help staff members to think for themselves by asking questions instead of giving answers
★ Measure every staff members performance via one or two Key Performance Indicators
★ Exit team members quickly and effectively when they are not meeting expectations

In order to achieve this, I recommend leaders in the business stop thinking of themselves as managers and instead view their role as coaches to their team members. The primary job of a manager is to get the most out of the people they support, the people who report to them. One of the most effective ways I have found to achieve this is to make anyone in the business who has direct reports accountable for the success of their team using the KPI 'percentage of team members who achieve their goals'. This forces them to focus on coaching team members.

Within the Accountability section, we'll look at the five key elements leaders need to implement in their business to have both internal and external accountability, and, along with the Ambassadorial role, will drive you towards having a higher percentage of top performers.

Key points

★ Good intentions toward staff can sometimes result in reduced responsibility from staff

★ Studies have demonstrated that as you add people to a team, the force exerted per person is reduced between five to ten percent per person

★ A key part of accountability is helping the person become more responsible

★ This responsibility can be achieved through insightful questioning, Key Performance Indicators and creating consequences when appropriate

Key Resources

★ "Who's got the monkey?" - Harvard Business Review November 1974 - William Oncken Jr.

★ https://www.spring.org.uk/2009/05/social-loafing-when-groups -are-bad-for-productivity

★ "Social loafing in wolf packs" - https://academic.oup.com/beheco /article/23/1/75/233162

1.1 All employees understand every aspect of what it takes to succeed in their role

Principle

Imagine you agree to join a friend's social hockey team. Like me perhaps, you know the basics of hockey – that there are goals, hockey sticks and a ball – but you don't know the rules, and you certainly don't understand the nuances within the game and the plays of your new team. You arrive for your first game eager to make new friends and stay fit, but very quickly you realise that it is very difficult to understand this new environment. For you to be successful, it would take a lot of learning, practice, and you see that some of your teammates and opponents are highly skilled, experienced and understand every aspect of what it takes to win a game. You may have the capability to play competitive hockey, and you may want to play competitive hockey; however, unless you understand every aspect of what it takes to win a game, you are unable to succeed.

In developing the accountability side of your business, it's crucial that you ensure every employee understands exactly what is expected of them and what it takes for them to succeed in their role, to the point where it is not possible to misunderstand what they must do to succeed.

This is the uncomfortable truth that many leaders are reluctant to admit. When I work with leadership teams and determine the people who are not performing, we dig down and ask why the person in question isn't performing as expected by asking three key questions:

1. Are they capable of succeeding in the role?
2. Do they understand what it takes to succeed in the role?
3. Do they want to succeed in the role?

The reason it is an uncomfortable truth is that many times we identify that the employee actually doesn't understand what it takes to succeed in the role to the point where it is not possible to misunderstand. Of the three questions, this is the question that most speaks to the leader's effectiveness in setting the person up for success.

It is simply unfair for a leader to fail to empower employees to succeed by not giving them an understanding of how to succeed in the organisation.

And yet it is by far the greatest obstacle to building accountability. If people aren't completely clear on how to succeed, it is hypocritical to hold them accountable when they fail to succeed.

In order to have employees in a position where it is not possible to misunderstand how to succeed, you must broadly focus on two areas: the productivity expectations and the culture or Core Values expectations.

For productivity it's important to have two Key Performance Indicators (KPIs) for each person, which I will detail in the next section. However, there are also other, important things people would need to do in order to achieve these KPIs. Now to be clear, we would not only want to measure the two KPIs per role in order to provide absolute focus for the employee, but we would also need the person to be aware of *how* to succeed in his or her role.

As an example, for a salesperson the KPI's might be:

KPI 1 - Number of meetings per week
KPI 2 - Sales $ per week

So, a successful week might look like 15 sales meetings and $20,000 in sales.

To provide that level of clarity to a salesperson and measure his or her weekly KPIs is a good start, but there could be another ten things that the person must do in order to achieve these goals consistently, such as:

★ Document every customer interaction in the Customer Relationship Management database

★ Call back all customers within 24 hours, identifying buying urgency on that call

★ Attend internal marketing meetings once per month to learn of new initiatives

★ Attend internal operational meetings once per month to understand operational issues

★ Don't leave more than two months between customer contact

★ Follow every step of our sales process and seek coaching weekly on current opportunities from the sales manager

★ Always present proposals to clients in person, never via email

★ Attend every sales training session provided

★ If you find yourself unlikely to achieve your weekly sales target by Wednesday afternoon, ask the sales manager for help, she always has a few opportunities

★ Build rapport with other sales reps, keeping a tally of lead exchanges

Or there could be fifty things the salesperson needs to do to achieve his or her KPIs. The number doesn't matter. It is the job of the leader to ensure that people understand how to succeed. That doesn't necessarily mean you need to do it yourself, but you need to be confident it happens.

When it comes to culture, once your Core Values are alive, consider a regular rhythm of Core Values stories as discussed in chapter three on culture, then discuss with the person what does it mean to actually live these Values? How do you live these Core Values on a regular basis?

For the sales person mentioned above, it's important to remember that if the person consistently achieves their sales targets, but is often in breach of the Core Values or cultural expectations, this person is not successful. If he or she can't make both the productivity and cultural expectations, they need to leave.

To help the salesperson understand Core Values, you can reference past Core Values stories or build a list of items outlining what it means to live the organisation's Values. We'll discuss Core Values stories and breaches more in chapter three.

Story

For Gene Browne and City Bin, his Galway, Ireland based waste collection firm, finding a way to help employees understand every aspect of their roles that contribute to their success was a focus in 2015. The company devoted an entire month to detailing the behaviours that were cool and the behaviours that were not.

There were 31 behaviours – one for each day of the month (16 Cool and 15 Not Cool) – that were intended to drive up City Bin's employee satisfaction and engagement, measured by the employee Net Promoter Score (eNPS). The relevant behaviour was highlighted during each daily huddle, and a daily email was sent to each staff member highlighting that day's Cool, Not Cool message.

According to Browne at the time: 'The theme is going down very well. The biggest difference I see now is that it's much easier to have that "awkward" conversation with a colleague. All you have to say is "Not Cool" and the message is understood.'

City Bin Cool / Not Cool theme

DAY	COOL FOCUS	DAY	NOT COOL FOCUS
1	Attention to detail	2	Long call waiting times
3	Delivering exceptional service	4	Not wearing your uniform
5	Solving the problem	6	Not putting the bins back
7	Respect for your colleagues	8	Gossip and politics
9	Respect for the customer	10	Bins not collected
11	Clean cabs and vehicles	12	Carelessness
13	Delivering Wow's	14	Passing the buck
15	Having some fun	16	Choosing to do 'drama'
17	Haul or call	18	Taking shortcuts
19	Crews in full uniform	20	Not getting back to customers
21	Helping a colleague under pressure	22	Untidy truck or desk
23	Seeing things from the customers viewpoint	24	Thinking 'us' versus 'them'
25	Taking pride in your work	26	Wasting time, money or energy
27	Getting it right first time	28	Not pulling your weight
29	Speaking up	30	Arguing with a customer
31	Owning the situation		

Tool

When CEOs react to poor performance within their team, they are often asking the wrong question. What they often ask is, 'how can I get that person to perform, maybe I should give them some more training or coaching or some more discipline'? I think that this is the wrong question.

I think the right question is not what can be done to improve the person, but why are they not performing in the first place?

The reason an employee isn't performing can be determined by returning to and answering these three questions:

1. Is the person capable of succeeding in the role?
2. Does the person understand how to succeed in the role?
3. Does the person want to succeed in the role?

So, if someone is capable of succeeding in the role, they are able to handle all of the requirements of the role both now and into the future. If the company doubled in size, they would still be able to handle all of the needs of the role without any problem.

If someone understands how to succeed in the role, they should know every single thing that it takes to succeed. They should know the KPIs, and relative to those KPIs quantitatively at what point they are doing a good job, what point they are doing a great job, and at what point they are failing and are close to receiving a warning for poor performance. Also, they should have a complete understanding of the cultural aspects of the role, a deep understanding of the Core Values and Core Purpose along with how that applies to certain circumstances. Finally, they should understand the complete job description for their role and any other metrics or actions they or their team need to do in order to succeed. Every single little thing they need to do in order to succeed in the role to the point where it's not possible for them to misunderstand.

Do they want to succeed in the role? Is the person just waiting for the weekend? Do they have a job because they just need to pay the bills, or do they really want to win at this job?

Now take a look at the table below and consider the employees who are not performing, placing their names in column 1 as shown in the first example. Next, on a scale of 1 to 10, rate each person, where 1 equals not at all and 10 equals absolutely. Remember that in this context, performing means living the Core Values and achieving the productivity results at the required level consistently.

Sample CUW table

NAME	CAPABLE OF SUCCEEDING	UNDERSTAND HOW TO SUCCEED	WANT TO SUCCEED	TOTAL
Employee 1	8	6	7	21
Employee 2	7	7	9	23
Employee 3	10	6	9	25

CUW table

NAME	CAPABLE OF SUCCEEDING	UNDERSTAND HOW TO SUCCEED	WANT TO SUCCEED	TOTAL

If you are capable of doing the role, and you understand the role, but you don't want to do it, it's not going to work.

If you understand the role, and you want to do the role, but you are not capable of doing the role, it's not going to work. If you are capable of doing the role, and you want to do the role, but you don't understand the expectations of the role, it's not going to work.

Now consider that last one. If someone doesn't understand the expectations of the role, but is capable and wants to succeed in the role, well there is an opportunity to help them to understand the role. But that work has to be put in. It is incumbent on you to make them so clear on what needs to be done in the role that it is not possible for them to misunderstand how to succeed.

Once you have rated each of your people from 1-10 against these three categories of capability, understand and want with a possible total score of 30, what did each person score? From this assessment, you should be able to target your coaching to each person. In particular, you should be able to see where to focus your next performance discussion.

You should be aiming for an average of your entire team to be over a score of 25. Because if you don't have an average of 25 for people who are capable, understand the role and want to do the role, you won't be able to grow. The teams that I work with that are thriving – well all of those people are above 25. And all of the teams I work with that struggle have an average below 25.

Key points

★ In order to succeed, staff must be capable of succeeding in their role, they must understand how to succeed in their role and they must want to succeed in their role.

★ Often the greatest obstacle to building accountability is that people aren't completely clear on how to succeed in their role

★ Succeeding in a role means both meeting the desired numbers and adhering to the Core Values or cultural expectations

Key Resources

★ www.citybin.com

1.2 All employees report to their peers weekly on the two KPIs which define their role

Principle

In his book, *The 5 Dysfunctions of a Team*, Patrick Lencioni outlined the five elements that contribute to effective teamwork. Lencioni found that in order to succeed, teams need to build trust, master healthy conflict, achieve commitment, embrace peer to peer accountability and focus on team results.

Having performed Lencioni's 5 Dysfunctions assessment with many teams, I have found the fourth requirement, to 'embrace peer to peer accountability' is the one which ranks as the lowest most of the time. And yet to achieve peer accountability within your team, to achieve an environment where team members call their peers on performance or behaviours which may hurt the team is the gold standard to aim for and the most effective environment to achieve results. In this environment team members don't rely on the leader as the primary source of accountability, but rather go directly to their peers.

This doesn't mean that the leader has no role in a team with peer accountability, instead the leader must confront difficult situations the rest of the team won't. Instead of being the primary arbiter, he or she must be the ultimate arbiter.

Imagine you are in a weekly meeting with five of your team members. One of the team members is not going to achieve his or her KPIs for the third week in a row. Are they reporting to you about the failure or are they reporting to the team? Are they more concerned about letting you down or letting the leadership team down? Are they concerned, period, or just providing a status update? If they're challenged by you or by peers at all, might they just reply with an excuse?

In a culture of peer accountability, the person would be reporting to the team, and several of the team members would be holding the failing team member to account without hesitation. It simply wouldn't be acceptable to have a co-worker not achieving prescribed tasks, projects and standards of performance. Several team members would be asking why the team member was not achieving their KPI's and enquiring about the plan to turn around the results in the coming week. Importantly they also would be asking if the person needs help to achieve their targets, providing both accountability to team members as well as support.

Finally, it removes the undue burden on the team leader to be the sole source of discipline. Evolving the way team members think and act toward one another isn't something you can change overnight, but by applying the peer accountability tools from *The 5 Dysfunctions of a Team* consistently over many quarters, I have seen some great turn-arounds in the way teams interact.

A simple tool to use in situations where team members are reluctant to hold one another accountable is the phrase 'Silence is complicity'. This is used to remind team members that if they don't speak up about something they might not agree with, then they are in fact agreeing that it's OK. Of course, this only works when each leadership team member prioritises the leadership team's collective results over individual or department needs. The leadership team needs to be their number one team; their department, career, ego or status should come second to this. Once team members are treating the leadership team as their number one team, it becomes much easier to call out other team members.

Of course, there is no point in working to develop a culture of peer accountability if there isn't a measurable focus on what must be achieved.

Have you ever seen a job advertisement where a list of ten or twelve KPIs are included? Where should the successful candidate focus? It's simply not going to be possible to focus on all twelve areas at once. If a person achieves four of the twelve but fails on the other eight, should they be fired? How about if they consistently achieve ten of the twelve? Are they failing then?

I have found that by setting more than two or three KPIs for a role, you are setting the person up to fail from the outset. Your job is to create the framework for people to succeed, and then to coach and support them to achieve success.

The best way to achieve a high level of focus is to determine two KPIs per role and per department that people can relentlessly focus on. Then set between three and five Specific, Measurable, Achievable, Realistic and Time-bound (SMART) priorities for each team and person to focus on for a quarter.

That's it.

Remove the distractions, bottlenecks and unnecessary reports. Always have the most important thing being the most important thing.

I would recommend the Function Accountability Chart or FACe tool developed by Verne Harnish and detailed in the book *Scaling Up: How a Few Companies Make It... and Why the Rest Don't* to which I was a contributor, for more information. The FACe tool helps to determine the leading and lagging KPI for each role in the business, and I find it to be so important to achieve this clarity per role, that it's something I always work with on day one with new clients.

A note on reducing the number of KPIs in a role for those who are worried that things will get missed and they could be blindsided: as we look across the business in mapping KPIs, our goal is to become metaphorically watertight. When we are watertight, important measurable indicators are not missed because someone is accountable for them. This means that if you had every role and department in the organisation reporting weekly on their two KPIs, and we had achieved this watertight state, there would be no need for unnecessary reports (that often aren't read anyway!).

Story
One of my businesses was a communications, electrical and IT company called Total Connect where I knew we had to have the right information

to sustain our growth rates, which were at times more than 80% per year, so I hired an accountant rather than a bookkeeper in the very early days, and I had the accountant develop a comprehensive reporting system so that we could see all the numbers we ever wanted to in the business. I found a list of KPIs and tried to track as many of the most relevant ones as I could.

This was in the early 2000s, and the business analytics tools weren't anywhere near as good as they are today, so my accountant would compile monthly reports that over the years became larger and more complex. One day I began to question the usefulness of these reports when I realised it was taking days and days of her time each month, and the monthly report had become a fifty-page beast!

Even worse, when I was getting the reports, I wasn't really reading them, and the information created wasn't really being used. I was just looking at a few key numbers and how a few other numbers were tracking.

So I began to think that I could double the number of KPIs in the report, or halve them and it wouldn't make any difference at all, except to the workload of the people creating the report. But the real problem was that I was getting the report monthly, when it was already too late, and the numbers weren't really getting down to the people who were accountable for them.

I realised that I needed to get fewer numbers, which were the right numbers, at the right time, to the right people. Then I needed to get people to focus on these two numbers and hold people accountable to the results they achieved.

Now, fifteen years later, this is still what I use as the framework for accountability within teams. Two KPIs per role and per department, ideally reported weekly to peers. No more creation of excessive reports that aren't even read. Less reporting, with a stronger focus and account-ability on the numbers that are reported.

Tool

Once you have determined what the leading and lagging KPIs are for each role, it's the 'meeting rhythm' another term from Harnish's *Scaling Up,* that becomes the glue that makes everything stick and ultimately work. The meeting rhythm is a disciplined framework of daily, weekly, monthly, quarterly and annual meetings, all with a set agenda to maintain the habit of stepping outside the day-to-day operations of the business to be able to undertake strategic thinking, execution planning and review performance. By implementing the meeting rhythm with one of my clients, we were able to stop holding forty-seven regularly scheduled meetings between leadership team members alone! We will discuss the details of the meeting rhythm later in this book.

Once you understand the principles of the meeting rhythm, ensure that one of the weekly agenda items is the review of key numbers. This means spending time having each team member report to the remainder of the team on how they are progressing on their two KPIs and their three to five priorities.

Generally, KPIs represent a person or team working 'in' the business, while priorities represent a person or team working 'on' the business, improving it in some way. So, a sales manager's KPI might be to achieve 100% of their sales budget (working *in* the business). However, a priority for the quarter could be to launch a new sales process (working *on* the business).

Within the meeting rhythm, as these KPIs and priorities are determined at a quarterly or annual meeting, the weekly meeting shouldn't be distracted by new opportunities – it is simply an update on how each person and department is performing. In the seven days after an offsite quarterly or annual workshop I like to have each leadership team member build a 13-week execution plan with their team that clearly demonstrates how they will achieve their KPIs and priorities in the coming quarter.

This way, when each team member is reporting at the weekly meeting, they are answering three important questions about their two KPIs and their three to five priorities.

What are the numbers from the last week on this KPI or priority - how am I tracking against my 13-week plan, am I Green (complete), Amber (on track) or Red (behind and urgently needs action)?

What do I need to do on this KPI or priority in the next seven days (our next weekly meeting)?

What have I done in the past seven days compared to what I said I was going to do?

The table below outlines how you can update each of these. You can also see very clearly the accountability where the person in week 1 said they were going to make 12 calls in the next 7 days, yet only made 8 calls.

It's one thing to have team members focussed and accountable on the right numbers. It's another to have the regular reporting and discussion of these numbers embedded into a habit within the business. Finally, it's yet another to have the team holding each other accountable to successes or failures within the business. Once you have all three operating effectively, the team can produce significantly better results and pulse faster.

KPI / Priority tracker

SMART GOAL TO BE TRACKED	E.G. SALES CALLS			
	PLANNED PROGRESS	ACTUAL PROGRESS TOWARD TOTAL	LAST 7 DAYS	NEXT 7 DAYS
Week 1	6	6	6	Increase to 12 to catch up
Week 2	12	14	8	Increase to 16 to catch up
Week 3	12			
Week 4	12			
Week 5	12			
Week 6	12			
Week 7	12			
Week 8	12			
Week 9	12			
Week 10	12			
Week 11	12			
Week 12	12			
Week 13	12			
End of quarter target	150 sales calls			

Key points

★ Many leaders struggle to create an environment of peer-to-peer accountability, an environment where the leader isn't the primary arbiter, but where he or she is the ultimate arbiter. This peer-to-peer accountability team dynamic creates better results.

★ It is better to set two or three Key Performance Indicators to measure performance in a person's role rather than many KPIs to ensure they have focus and provide managers with clearer points of accountability.

★ You should aim to track fewer numbers, which are the right numbers, and provide them at the right time, to the right people. Then get people to focus on these numbers and hold people accountable to the results they achieve.

Key Resources

★ *The 5 Dysfunctions of a Team* - Patrick Lencioni

★ *Scaling Up: How a Few Companies Make It... and Why the Rest Don't* - Verne Harnish

1.3 Failure has a consequence that is transparent and is known by all employees and suppliers

Principle

Cameron Herold was one of the lecturers at the Entrepreneurial Masters Program I attended at MIT in conjunction with the Entrepreneurs Organization, and author of the books *Double Double* and *Meetings Suck*. Cam was the former COO at '1800 Got Junk' and helped delegates to identify the people in their business who didn't align with Core Values and were not productive in their roles. Once the class had rated our high, middle and low performers we faced the confrontational part, when he asked each of us to fire the lowest-rated staff members within a week of our return back to our businesses. Ouch.

Why was it so difficult to do when we knew they were not the right people for the job anyways?

On reflection, we hadn't appreciated the cost of keeping the wrong people when we believed that they could improve, despite all the evidence suggesting otherwise. According to Brad Smart's research, outlined in his book *Topgrading: The Proven Hiring and Promoting Method That Turbocharges Company Performance*, the cost of not taking action on poor performers is actually much higher than people expect. An entry level role mis-hire can cost a business as much as the person's annual salary, while an executive mis-hire can cost twenty-five times the person's annual salary!

The reasons for these mis-hire costs include the real dollar hiring costs, lost productivity and the organisational damage.

Of course, this doesn't only apply to productivity KPIs for employees. Core Values breaches can do just as much damage to team morale. If you have a staff member who doesn't align with the Core Values and is consistently creating cultural challenges, they should be reprimanded or terminated. See Chapter 3 on culture for more on this.

Equally, suppliers and subcontractors must be clear on their performance expectations. It is easy to assume that they will perform or you will move your business to another company, but we all know that many subcontractor and supplier relationships have problems with both performance and Core Values breaches. Therefore, it's important to make clear to suppliers and subcontractors exactly what they must achieve in terms of productivity and which Values are important to you.

Just like employees, often suppliers and subcontractors will not be aware what they need to do in order to maintain preferred status. It is your job to ensure they are completely clear about this to the point that it is not possible for them to misunderstand your expectations.

Do you need to be a mean-spirited boss, the one who yells and screams to get the results they want? No. As outlined in the previous section, the most effective environment to create results is one where all team members hold each other accountable, rather than there being a sole source of accountability. However, you are responsible for creating this culture of peer accountability, it won't happen simply on its own. See Patrick Lencioni's *The 5 Dysfunctions of a Team* for more details.

Building an environment with consequence being the natural reaction to poor performance is fundamentally important to creating a great company. If you tolerate mediocrity, the result will be a mediocre company.

Story

For me, the word consequence has a deeper meaning.

About a dozen years ago, I was having quality problems in my business that were incredibly frustrating. Staff were not taking the care that seemed necessary. Customers were complaining, and we couldn't understand why the systems we were so proud of were failing.

So, I decided to take my leadership team away for a planning session at a country retreat to understand exactly what was happening by breaking the problem down into parts and with hope, leaving with clarity and the problem solved.

Of course it didn't end up being that easy.

Over two days, about six of us broke all the problems down into root causes. At the end we analysed the common thread across all these issues. After intense thinking, breaking down the problem into its sub parts to search for the reasons it came down to one word, consequence. I had just spent two days and more than ten thousand dollars to drive home from the country with one word, consequence. Ouch again.

I learned that I had built a culture where leaders and middle managers didn't want to create a consequence when a staff member failed to deliver. By consequence, I don't only mean termination. I mean anything, even sitting down and working through why it happened with the staff member.

Without consequences for mistakes and problems, staff didn't learn from those mistakes. They felt that management didn't care, and that made them care even less about results.

We learned from this mistake and ensured that every problem had a consequence. Our leaders actively engaged with problems and closed the loop on issues we learned about. We talked with staff when something happened. We warned staff. We even sacked staff. We demonstrated through our actions that we cared about failure.

The result was people started to care more, problems decreased and customer complaints dropped.

Ensuring that there is a clear and transparent consequence for employees and suppliers, that you are not the sole source of consequence isn't easy, but it is vitally important.

Tool

Think about the last few times an employee or supplier has failed to deliver. I'm sure a few examples come to mind pretty quickly.

On the tool below, in the left column, write the situation.

Next, describe how the business suffered. Perhaps you lost a client, lost money or suffered reputational damage.

In the third column, answer who was the person accountable. Not more than one person either, –narrow it down to who is the single person who failed in his or her duty.

In the fourth column, write down what the actual consequence that person suffered as a result of the situation was.

Finally answer the following question: given the manner in which the business suffered, what consequence would prevent that person taking this action in the future?

Then try think of a few other situations where people have failed to deliver and complete the four columns for these situations.

In the future, when you have an employee or supplier fail, ask yourself, 'What is the consequence that would prevent this occurring again'?

Of course sacking an employee shouldn't be your only answer, and I certainly encourage you to comply with employment and dismissal laws in your country.

Often times simply having a one on one meeting to express your disappointment may be appropriate. One of the simplest accountability tools I learned was from the Police Commissioner in our state. I imagine he has many situations where he needs simple consequence tools. His simple and effective tool was asking the question, 'Can you help me to understand?' It cuts through all the excuses, diversions and tactics used by skilled consequence avoiders and gets straight to the uncomfortable point. But equally important, it implies that I have come to expect more from you and perhaps I don't have all the information!

Let's look at the question in action with a few examples:

'Can you help me understand why you conducted yourself in an unprofessional manner during that meeting'?'

'Can you help me understand why you were seen at the bar when you called in sick?'

Consequence analysis

Situation	How the business suffered	Person accountable	Actual consequence	Consequence for the person accountable that would prevent this action occurring again

'Can you help me to understand why you failed to test that product in accordance with our standards?'

Remember, if you have to sack the person, you have failed, and you have thousands of opportunities before this time arises to be able to correct the person's behaviours using smaller consequences rather than major consequences like sacking them. It's useful to build up a mental list of micro consequences over time to deal with these types of situations.

You'll find a few on the next page to start.

There are hundreds of other consequences that you can create. The problem is that so many leaders want to be friends with their employees, or at least be liked. They don't want to be seen as the mean boss. Yet in actual fact you are failing in your duty to them if you do not create a consequence for employees. You are preventing them from learning the valuable lessons to help them grow, and you are sending a message to their co-workers that it is acceptable to fail.

Let me say that again. In each of the situations you outlined in the table above where employees failed and you didn't create a consequence, you sent a message to other team members that you find that situation acceptable.

They interpret that to mean that you just don't care.

They will need to work late to catch up	They work on the weekend	Have a special meeting with you	Have a special meeting with your boss
Cancel, reduce or delay their bonus	They create a diary outlining what they are doing through the day	They create an action plan to turnaround the situation	Special chat every morning to update their progress
They can build a better system and present it to you	They do a root cause analysis	They don't get to work on the best tasks	Silence when you are questioning them. Make the conversation uncomfortable
Tell them you are disappointed	Explain how their performance puts the whole business or department performance in jeopardy	Ask them to report back to you in 24 hours with an update on a turnaround	Ask what they would do different and what they will do in the next 7 days to improve

Key points

* ★ Employees, suppliers and subcontractors should be clear on your expectations.
* ★ Major or minor failures to meet these expectations should result in an appropriate consequence.
* ★ Many leaders interpret consequence as meaning only dismissal, whereas it can be as simple as expressing verbal disappointment.
* ★ The absence of consequence sends a message that you don't really care, whether it is your intention or not.

Key Resources

* ★ *Double Double* - Cameron Herold
* ★ *Meetings Suck* - Cameron Herold
* ★ *Topgrading: The Proven Hiring and Promoting Method That Turbocharges Company Performance* - Bradford Smart
* ★ *The 5 Dysfunctions of a Team* - Patrick Lencioni

1.4 All team meetings are conducted with an agenda and data is available to effectively make decisions during meetings

Principle

Meetings Suck!

That's the title to one of the books written by Cam Herold, whom I mentioned in the last section.

Cam's simple premise is that we spend around 20% of our time in meetings and most people don't find meetings valuable. In fact, when you consider the hourly salary of each attendee, the average meeting costs between $500 and $1,000, and many people walk away thinking, 'What a waste of my time!'

In your business, how do you maintain the quality of meetings?

Quality of meetings held by all team members is an important area to consider when looking at how to make your team both as efficient and effective as possible. This is not only about you wasting your time attending ineffective meetings, this is about everyone, because your impact is governed by your ability to leverage your team.

As Verne Harnish wrote in *Mastering the Rockefeller Habits: What You Must Do to Increase the Value of Your Growing Firm* the key to successful execution is found by having the right priorities, the right metrics and data along with a consistent meeting rhythm which is disciplined, involving daily, weekly, monthly, quarterly and annual meetings.

It's the discipline that really matters. Even down to starting on time. Verne recommends starting daily huddles at an irregular time, such as 8.52 a.m. instead of 9.00 a.m., to ensure discipline. Another important factor in discipline is to ensure that attendees attend. If you are needed at an important meeting, you shouldn't be skipping it. Maybe ask team members to dial in if they're unavailable, but it isn't acceptable to not attend because you are working.

One of the great statesmen of my home state of Western Australia was the former premier Sir Charles Court. His philosophy when it comes to meetings was, '*if you aren't ten minutes early, you are late!*' What a great way to set the importance and expectations upfront! I also had the opportunity to sit on a board with a successful local businessman who was chairing the meetings for the organisation. Every single meeting would end within one minute of the close time on the agenda. If the meeting was due to close at 5.00, he would be providing his closing comments at 4.59. Contrast this with another board I sat on where there wasn't an agenda and meetings would always run 30 to 60 minutes over time.

Of course, this level of discipline can only be maintained if team members aren't attending an excessive number of meetings. The key is to hold less meetings in a regular rhythm with a strict agenda, more focussed preparedness by attendees, and the readily available information to make decisions on the spot. Everything slows down when people aren't prepared for a meeting. If you're the leader holding a meeting with your team to talk about their department or perhaps progress on a project, how long is it taking them to prepare for that meeting? Perhaps five or ten minutes? What would be different during that meeting if they spent two hours preparing instead? How would the quality of the discussions and the decisions made be different? Now I'm not suggesting that all your team should spend two hours preparing for a meeting with you, but I am asking you to consider the difference in quality when people are genuinely prepared.

If you are looking for a simple way to start increasing discipline around a messy meeting schedule, the simple phrase from *Meetings Suck* is 'No Agenda No Attenda'. It's a tool that anyone can use to define whether or not they will attend meetings and it explicitly states that if you don't provide an agenda for the meeting you are requesting I attend, which clearly outlines what will be discussed, how I need to prepare and how long it will take, then I will not attend. My time is more valuable than your lack of preparation.

No Agenda, No Attenda; I love it!

Story

I had been working with a business for a couple of years coaching and facilitating their strategic planning workshops. The work we had done was accelerating growth, and people were beginning to feel like they didn't have enough time to get things done. Of course, people's thoughts quickly turned to the need for more resources instead of trying to make the resources we had more effective.

This consideration for more resources made us ask, 'How do we know we need more resources? What is the data that proves this is true?'

From here we assessed who was busy, and why. This involved assessing the OPJs (Other People's Jobs) they were doing as well as the meetings they were attending that prevented them from doing their job.

When we went through the leadership team, we found that there were forty-seven meetings being held every week between leadership team members. No meetings had an agenda, and they had a start time but not a finish time. Therefore, the best we could determine is they took one to two hours per meeting.

If we assume two people in each meeting, 47 meetings per week on 48 working weeks per year and 1.5 hours per meeting, they were spending 6,768 hours per year just meeting with one another!

We were able to cut this down to eight meetings per week with a longer, half-day meeting once per month. This reduced the hours spent in meetings per year from around 6,768 to around 1,152 by providing a disciplined meeting structure that included the right priorities, the right metrics and data to make decisions in meetings along with the proper meeting rhythm structure.

People had to come prepared with the right information and opinions on subjects being discussed. We built a specific agenda for every meeting and then validated that our rhythm was 'watertight' and that important things wouldn't be missed.

They weren't.

The leadership team's efficiency and effectiveness increased significantly. The combination of them being able to have more time to actually do their job, along with the effectiveness of the meetings, which meant that decisions were being made and things were actually getting done a lot faster in the business, was transformative in their ability to grow.

Tool

How many regular meetings do you attend each week? Who requested the meeting, who is the chair and timekeeper?

Below are seven simple questions that lead to successful meetings. You should be able to answer yes to each of these questions.

- ★ Has the meeting organiser provided a detailed agenda with timings and including key subjects to be discussed?
- ★ Will decision makers be present in the meeting?
- ★ Have invitees been provided sufficient information and data to enter the room with a perspective on agenda items?
- ★ Will invitees come prepared?
- ★ Will all invitees provide a meaningful contribution to the meeting (or remain silent)?
- ★ Will invitees provide a return on their attendance greater than the cost of their attendance?
- ★ Will data be available during the meeting to ensure decisions are made and not postponed?

Now look at the regularly scheduled meetings in your calendar that you have each week and tick each box to determine whether the meeting is likely to be valuable or not. I've assumed that you are having no more than 3 regularly scheduled meetings per day, if you are then simply adapt the table as necessary.

Successful meeting planner

	Agenda with timing & subjects provided beforehand	Decision makers present	Data on subjects provided beforehand	Invitees coming prepared	All invitees contribute	All invitees ROI is positive	All data is available in the meeting
Monday #1							
#2							
#3							
Tuesday #1							
#2							
#3							
Wednesday #1							
#2							
#3							
Thursday #1							
#2							
#3							
Friday #1							
#2							
#3							

Key points

- ★ Meetings can be a very expensive and inefficient cost that leaders often ignore.
- ★ Also, meetings can be very frustrating for attendees if not effective.
- ★ Providing a formal meeting structure for the company to distribute information and make decisions can be the most effective way to reduce this cost and frustration.
- ★ All meetings should have an agenda provided beforehand for delegates to review.
- ★ All delegates should come prepared with data and information to enable decisions to be made in the meeting.

Key Resources

- ★ *Meetings Suck* - Cameron Herold
- ★ *Mastering the Rockefeller Habits: What You Must Do to Increase the Value of Your Growing Firm* - Verne Harnish

1.5 Internal and external employees and suppliers who do not consistently perform are rapidly removed from the business

Principle

Earlier in this chapter, I outlined how failure needs to have a consequence otherwise people won't learn. This doesn't necessarily mean dismissal, but without consequence, ideally drawn from a culture of peer-to-peer accountability, leaders will encourage mediocrity and place an undue burden on the leader as the sole source of discipline.

While failure must have a consequence, consistent failure must lead to dismissal. As Ron Shaich, CEO of Panera Bread the US-based bakery-café restaurants with over 2,000 locations says, 'I didn't come fully into my own as a leader until the past 10 years of my career. Now I see my mistake. I didn't understand that a leader can't put up with employees' baloney. If someone isn't producing, a leader has a right and an obligation to fire them.'

'Eventually I learned that servant leadership isn't about being nice at all costs. It's about being helpful at all costs. A leader should be as brutally honest as possible – and you can do this in a kind and loving way. Let the chips fall where they may, and remember: Honesty is helpful. When you tell someone why they're doing a bad job, you're transferring the responsibility. Maybe they improve. Maybe they leave. Whatever the outcome, they own it.'

In his 1997 book, *The War for Talent*, McKinsey & Company consultants Ed Michaels, Helen Handfield-Jones and Beth Axelrod surveyed more than 13,000 senior executives at 120 companies and found that only 19% felt their companies removed low performers quickly and effectively. The book went on to say that this failure to take action not only impacts the productivity of the business, but has a significant effect on the ability of an organisation to attract and retain high performers.

But *The War for Talent* survey was conducted in large enterprise organisations with extensive resources and HR departments. There is every chance that your business is smaller than these, and it is likely that staff in your organisation might not be so generous.

Imagine you were tasked to run a professional sports team. In order to win the championship you need to have the best possible player in every position. Every player needs to earn his or her spot and consistently prove that he or she is indeed capable of winning a championship.

If 25% of your team was unable to achieve the required statistics to retain their spot on the team, let alone be the best at their position on the field, you wouldn't stand a chance at winning the championship. Pretty quickly your plan would become to exit the players who weren't consistently performing and replace them with fantastic new players who would consistently exceed the statistics for their role on the team.

Which team wouldn't stand a chance at winning the championship? The team which failed to exit players rapidly and who tolerated poor performance consistently. The team that wouldn't stand a chance is the ones who kept players on the team because they were liked by teammates, were friendly or were coach favorites.

Yet this is what happens in a majority of businesses every single day. Leaders tolerate poor performers for long periods of time and fail to exit them from the business, thereby jeopardising the ability for the business to 'win' against its competition.

However, that isn't the extent of the problem. In your sports team, the real stars, the ones who are the best in the game for their position, look across at these consistently failing team mates with disdain. They believe that they are not winning games because of their teammates. Your failure to exit these poor performers has one or two effects on the top performers. Their performance drops, or they leave the team to find a team who are capable of winning the championship. It is extremely demotivating for top performers to be surrounded by poor performers.

Of course, it's exactly the same in your organisation. If you aren't regularly exiting poor performers, then the overall team performance suffers, the top performer's output drops and they are demotivated, or they leave to work at an organisation they feel will make their effort worthwhile. In exactly the same way you want to make your effort count for the most, so do top performers.

In fact you owe it to those in your organisation who are the best and brightest to surround them with similar people. Don't let their drive and capability go to waste. They want to do amazing things, and if you don't remove poor performers quickly and effectively, you are doing a lot more than just financial damage.

Story

Jo runs a successful business with around 100 employees and a sales staff of two. While most sales come to the business through word of mouth, and repeat business orders go directly into Jo's system for fulfilment, her two sales people bring in new business outside of the inbound sales the business already enjoys.

Two years ago Jo employed her first sales person to grow the business. She had founded the business many years earlier and built up her clientele hustling and finding all new sales herself. But she recognised that new client growth had slowed, and she simply didn't have the time to run the business and bring in new clients. So, Jo figured that employing a salesperson to focus on bringing in new clients was a good way to expand the business. With a little research, she determined that a salesperson was going to require a salary of $100k and based on this cost, they would need to sell $500k in Gross Profit – revenue minus her cost of materials – in order for the role to work and to profitably grow the business.

After a year, new sales growth hadn't been as good as Jo had hoped. Instead of the $500k Jo had planned for, the new salesperson had generated just over $340k GP in sales. She decided the best approach to achieve her new sales targets was to employ a second sales person.

The following year the first sales person had sold $360k and the second salesperson sold just under $290k. Of course, the salespeople had all manner of excuses, but the simple fact was that Jo's plan to grow new sales was 35% under budget across the two sales positions. By tolerating poor performance and not acting rapidly, Jo had incurred a $510k loss against her budget for the two years. But more than that, other workers in the business who knew that the salespeople were not achieving budget wondered why Jo hadn't acted.

The situation came to a head when one of Jo's friends asked about her new client sales team, and Jo expressed her disappointment. The friend challenged her, asking what she could do with $510k in other parts of her business. Within three weeks, Jo had fired both the sales people and was advertising for one new salesperson. She eventually found a salesperson who wanted a salary of $115k, which was more than she originally wanted to pay, but she was confident that this new salesperson could achieve the budget, and so she increased the budgets accordingly. Five months after starting, the new salesperson was selling 18% over budget.

Tool

Your goal should be to help people succeed in their role and to support people to be successful.

This means that your team members should be absolutely clear on what success looks like and what failure looks like.

Now it goes without saying that you must comply with employment law in your region, and I encourage you to be certain that you are within the law before taking any disciplinary action. In Australia, as an example, there are very strict laws that you must adhere to when firing a person that include clear, written information on what the employee must do and when in order to meet the role objectives and avoid dismissal. If you do not comply with these laws, the employee has the opportunity to lodge an unfair dismissal claim that can result in tens of thousands of dollars in payment to the former worker.

Sample return on investment calculator

	RETURN ON INVESTMENT FOR THE ROLE	KEY PERFORMANCE INDICATOR FOR THE ROLE	GREEN (BUDGET)	RED (UNACCEPTABLE)
SALESPERSON	5 x the salary in Gross Profit sales per month	Gross Profit sales per month	>$500k	<$250k
TECHNICIAN	2.5 x the salary in chargeable hours per month	Chargeable hours per month	>124	<100
MARKETING ASSOCIATE	50 x the salary in closable lead value per month	Closable leads per month	>$300k	<$225k

As frustrations build toward a failing employee, I have seen many CEOs say that they simply want to pay them out and make them leave. That they've just had enough. My response is always that paying someone to go or paying an unfair dismissal claim is not only lazy but sends a strong message to the remainder of your workforce that there is a lack of even-handed accountability at this firm.

If people are to understand your expectations of their role, they have to understand when, why and for what they could be fired. What will be the sequence of events that lead to dismissal?

Of course, in the first section of this chapter I made the case that you should be certain that employees understand every aspect of what it takes to succeed in their role using the Capable, Understand, Want tool before taking any disciplinary action.

In the second section of this chapter, I discussed how each team member needs to have two KPIs for their role, and how ideally they should be held accountable to these KPIs using peer accountability. As you will see in the chart below, before hiring for a role, it is important to consider the question, 'What is the Return On Investment I need from this role to make it a success?'

Only once you have a return on investment that aligns with your overall budget and is achievable for team members can you have a real appreciation just how much team members who don't perform are costing you. Why is this important? You should know how much their failure costs you, and, before they begin, the circumstances under which you would fire them. But most importantly, before they begin, they should know the number which will cause you to fire them.

This means drawing a 'line in the sand', determining exactly when it is time to fire someone, before they even arrive for their first job interview.

For example, in the chart above, the salesperson must produce >$500k Gross Profit, and <$250k is unacceptable. When should you fire this person?

>   After being $1m total under budget in a 12 month period?

>   After 4 consecutive months under budget?

>   After 1 quarter less than $750k Gross Profit?

>   I'll bet they want to know!

>   Pick a number for every role in your business. How much money do you want to lose when someone isn't performing? No excuses, no 'ifs,' no 'buts.'

Role return on investment calculator

ROLE E.G.	RETURN ON INVESTMENT FOR THE ROLE	KEY PERFORMANCE INDICATOR FOR THE ROLE	GREEN (BUDGET)	RED (UNACCEPTABLE)
Marketing				
Sales				
Operations				
Accounting				

As Ron Shaich from Panera Bread says above, you must be brutally honest in a kind and loving way. One way you can approach this difficult conversation is outlined in the manner below.

"If you fail to achieve budget for four consecutive months we must let you go. Don't get me wrong, we want you to be a superstar here and will provide all the tools, leads, training and coaching you need. But we are aiming for greatness and I'm sure you will understand that means we can't tolerate mediocrity"

If you wish to achieve consistent results along with a higher percentage of top performers, you must be clear when a role is failing to produce an acceptable return and when you should take action.

Key points

★ Effective leaders provide honest feedback about when and why people are not doing a good job.

★ Very few companies remove low performers quickly and effectively, however it is a leaders obligation to do so.

★ Top performers can't operate alongside poor performers. Their performance either drops or they leave.

★ It's important to identify the performance you expect from a role before you hire for that role, and the level at which you would fire someone. Also, a person employed in that role should be clear when they commence what that number is.

Key Resources

★ https://www.entrepreneur.com/article/308427 - "The Founder of Panera Bread: 'I Wish I'd Fired More People'"

★ *The War for Talent* - Harvard Business Review Press - Ed Michaels, Helen Handfield-Jones, and Beth Axelrod

★ AMBASSADOR

2.0 The CEO performs a strategic role as an ambassador

The word ambassador originally comes from the Latin word *ambactus*, meaning servant. Today the word ambassador relates to a person in a diplomatic capacity for a country or, 'a representative or promoter of a specified activity', which is the context we use it in this book.

Yet the original servant meaning isn't lost here.

Everyone serves someone. It's just some people don't like to believe they do.

If you are a politician you serve voters, and the sceptical amongst us would also say lobbyists.

If you work for yourself without employees, you serve your customers.

If you are an employee, you serve customers and your boss.

If you are a boss you serve your clients, shareholders and employees.

In his book *Ego is the Enemy: The Fight to Master Our Greatest Opponent*, Ryan Holiday outlined one of the obstacles to a servant mindset: 'Ego is the enemy of what you want and of what you have: Of mastering a craft,' he writes. 'Of real creative insight. Of working well with others. Of building loyalty and support. Of longevity. Of repeating and retaining your success. It repulses advantages and opportunities. It's a magnet for enemies and errors'.

I'm sure that like me, you have heard business owners proudly proclaim that 'they don't report to anyone' and you get a sense that perhaps to do so would be beneath them. Oddly enough, just like their peers, they also take calls from unhappy customers with problems, as well as staff with problems who are probably not happy.

We all serve somebody, like it or not.

What if that business owner reversed his or her thinking, checked his or her ego and instead of saying, 'I don't report to anyone,' said 'I serve our customers, staff and shareholders'?

How would it change their perspective? How would it change the actions they take? How would it change the results they achieve?

In another situation you may have experienced, business leaders grow frustrated because staff don't do everything the leader believes they should. 'I pay them, why do they always come to me with problems?', leaders may be left asking. 'They should do what I say.' The mindset here is that because they are paid, staff should have no problems, as if the money that is paid to staff should somehow make staff immediately subservient, like an English butler in a suit and gloves waiting on your every need during waking hours.

What if that business owner reversed his or her thinking, checked his or her ego and instead of asking 'Why don't they do what I say' asked 'How can I serve my employees'?

How would it change his or her perspective? How would it change the actions they take? How would it change the results they achieve?

For Darren Holland, CEO at Aventus, an owner and manager of large format retail centres with over half a million square metres across twenty showrooms throughout Australia, this perspective about serving and supporting the people, and the message that both he and the team who centrally manages the business demonstrate is that the administration centre is not called head office, but instead is known as the support office. This conscious decision is intended to communicate to the twenty centres that the administration centre exists to support each of the centres.

I'm certainly not suggesting you should do your employees jobs, far from it.

I am suggesting, however, that part of your role as the company ambassador is to help employees to do their job by adopting a serving or supporting mindset and promoting specific activities to both them and your customers.

If you approach your work with a mindset that you don't report to anyone, or that staff should be subservient, you will be less likely to be proactive in your actions toward employees, clients or shareholders. On the other hand, if you adopt a humble approach and consider that your ego is in fact the enemy, and that your job is indeed to serve customers, staff and shareholders you can begin to be proactive, allocate time to manage serving these stakeholders and build a system to be ambassadorial for each of these groups.

For this reason, a leader must allocate time to his or her strategic role as an ambassador. By allocating time to be an ambassador both inside and outside the company, being a promoter of who the business is, what the company plans and priorities are, and celebrating and welcoming new staff and new clients with a servant mindset, a leader will drive higher engagement, which will contribute toward a higher percentage of top performers and higher retention rates.

Key points

★ Every person is responsible for serving someone, in one form or another.

★ Accepting this fact, and adopting a humble mindset, endeavouring to do a good job of serving requires an understanding of how your ego can work against the outcomes you really want to achieve.

★ Serving as a great leader includes being an ambassador and promoter of the business to customers, shareholders, staff and suppliers.

Key Resources

★ *Ego is the Enemy: The Fight to Master Our Greatest Opponent* - Ryan Holiday

2.1 The CEO has a system to build a public profile such as industry forums, industry leadership, blogging or speaking

Principle

The 2018 Edelman Trust Barometer, a study of 33,000 people across 25 countries, stated that for CEOs the number one job is building trust in their company. It was more important than high quality products and services, business decisions reflecting company values and even profit and stock price increases.

A lack of public trust in a CEO damages the business they represent. The public begins to associate its negative perception of the leader's characteristics with the company as a whole.

Therefore, the public's trust in a business is dependant on its trust in the leader.

Fortunately you can build trust, and the best way is through transparency, simply telling the truth in a way that people can verify. People inherently don't want to mistrust a business. Instead they are trying to find businesses they trust in a world of fake news and mistrust. People actually want to hear genuine, authentic, transparent CEOs who are working to live both their companies purpose as well as create profits and shareholder value.

Of course, there is no point in being transparent all by yourself and not interacting with anyone. The entire purpose is to build a trusted public profile, to increase trust in the business.

Some CEOs desperately avoid attention and any form of public profile, and the reverse is true also. Some seek every opportunity to build their public profile. I know of a superannuation company that buys an advert in the Australian Financial Review newspaper every week with a full-page photo of the director. If that works for them and isn't your cup of tea, that's fine. But they do have a system to build a public profile, and I assure you they wouldn't be spending the tens of thousands of dollars every week they do unless it worked for them.

It's important to remember though, that the purpose is ambassadorial: it's to build a public profile, not to feed your ego or to increase sales. You're out to build trust, trust from the public, customers and suppliers as well as trust from your employees and stakeholders.

If you don't cultivate and control your public profile using a system, it's unlikely people will find your business authentic, which may create a barrier to trust.

A website with stock images and stock text purely designed to optimise SEO is just that, stock. Every time I come across a website like this it makes me wonder whether there are any real people in this company?

I suspect that I'm not alone when I say that I don't want to deal with a stock company. I want to deal with a company, supported by a leader that is honest and transparent in a way I can verify for myself if I want. I want to deal with companies I can *trust*. I don't care if they make mistakes, as long as they admit it and remain true to their transparency mandate.

Maybe you have no appetite to build a public profile. Perhaps you don't have a single social media account, and that's the way you like it. For you, that might mean that industry leadership would be more suitable such as volunteering on your industry association or contributing to an industry media publication.

As a CEO you are the custodian of the trust that people hold in your organisation. In order to positively impact your staff and in particular your top performers, and to achieve higher retention, staff need to have both pride in the organisation and trust. Both of these are impacted from the CEO acting in an Ambassadorial role.

Story

A few years ago I was in the market for a new car. Now I'm the type of person who does quite a bit of research, especially for something as expensive as a new car. If you have ever searched for a new car online, you're probably familiar with my dilemma. Visiting a new car website feels like you have stepped into a TV advertisement and they are trying to be as faceless and 'stock' as possible.

Sure, there were big banners telling me about the latest financing deal or what I could get if I bought in the next week, but that wasn't what I wanted to know. Those considerations would come much later in my buying cycle. I was there to build a relationship, to build trust.

But more than that, I wanted to know about the company, the cars and the people behind them. I am deeply passionate about business, and especially Australian business. For that reason, I wanted an Australian-made car. I wanted to see stories of the passionate people who built the car, stories of the quality people who undertook relentless testing and stories of the leaders who believed they were on a mission to build a world-class car. I didn't want to hear it from an anonymous marketing person. I wanted to hear it from them.

Unfortunately, six months later I started to hear those stories through the media when GM Holden announced they were closing their Australian manufacturing business within three years. I found out there were in fact real people in the business who were proud about building one of the best cars in the world. I always suspected these people were hidden in the factories, and now I knew as the media were interviewing them and telling their stories that I'd been right. Looking at their website though, I had found a faceless corporation with beautiful models in photoshopped images on long, windy roads. A faceless corporation is really difficult to trust.

It felt like there was an absence of ambassadorial conduct to positively drive transparency and build trust.

Looking at a new car website is a great way to experience what a dehumanised international corporation looks like, when no one is allowed to take a risk and be transparent.

I'm not suggesting that the reason GM Holden closed its

manufacturing facility was purely due to an absence of the CEO undertaking an ambassadorial role – there were many other political factors at play both in the U.S. and Australia – but I do claim that a trusted CEO, one who is transparent and genuine in building a great business, will have the support of a great many people both inside and outside the business.

Tool

In the chart below, consider what you could do to build your public profile.

You should only consider actions you are comfortable with, and you certainly can engage the help of a marketing or PR professional if it makes it easier for you, however it does need to be in your authentic 'voice'.

Begin by considering whether it is suitable in your situation and you are comfortable doing it. In the worth doing column place a yes or no.

Next, if you listed yes for the idea, who do you need to discuss the idea with to further it? Who would know more about this medium within your friends and contacts?

In the 'what I can do column', list your idea. At this point in time, what is your vision for the idea?

Finally, list when you can complete it by – this is your timeline. You don't need to build a complete project management chart, but is it an easy or hard goal? Starting a blog on your company website might be easy and achievable within a month. Finding speaking opportunities however can be much harder and might take much longer. Just make your best guess at this point.

One last note. As a filter, consider your credibility and commitment. If you passionately start a blog and promote it heavily for three months, then give up, will it affect your credibility? Are you committing to something you will stick to consistently and grow, gradually and over time, to improve your role as an ambassador? Be certain that any new initiative is one you are prepared to commit to.

Profile builder worksheet

IDEA	WORTH DOING YES / NO	WHO I NEED TO DISCUSS WITH	WHAT I CAN DO	WHEN I CAN COMPLETE
Blogging on your company website				
Blogging on others websites as a guest				
Video blogging (Vlogging)				
Writing articles on media sites				
Newsletter				
Social media - LinkedIn, Facebook, Twitter etc				
Speaking at industry events				
Speaking at events outside your industry				
Media quoting as an expert				
Industry leadership and volunteering				
Industry media publications				
Charity and not-for-profit work				

Key points

★ The public's trust in a business is dependant on its trust in the leader.

★ Leaders must manage their public profile with the aim to be an ambassador and build trust.

★ Building your public profile is very important as the primary ambassador, but it should be done in ways you are comfortable with.

Key Resources

★ Edelman Trust Barometer 2018 - https://www.edelman.com/trust-barometer

2.2 The CEO attends all major customer contract signings or product launches

Principle

I get it. You're busy.

You have a sales manager and a sales person whose job is to sell. To profitably manage customers. Why should you attend a contract signing or a product launch?

Because it's important. Because from the customers perspective and your staff's perspective, the CEO attending in an ambassadorial role acknowledges this importance.

As Tim Ferris, author of *The 4-Hour Work Week: Escape the 9-5, Live Anywhere and Join the New Rich* states, 'Being perpetually busy is a form of laziness. If you don't feel like you have time, you don't have priorities. It's very easy to confuse activity with productivity'.

Imagine two scenarios.

After months of research and work, you and your partner have decided to build a house. You have selected the builder and you go to their offices to sign the contract. All the documents are prepared, and you walk in, meet the sales person and sign the contract.

In the second scenario, the only difference is that you meet the sales person with the CEO of the company sitting in on the meeting. It's a half hour meeting, and the CEO simply says that your house is one of their larger and more-expensive homes. He says he wanted to spend the time to meet you, answer any last-minute questions you may have had in person and to make sure you were going to be looked after through the entire process.

As a customer, how do you feel about that CEO acting in an ambassadorial role?

I am sure that CEO was busy and could have been doing other things. But the priority of being an ambassador positively impacted both the salesperson and you, the client.

Of course, every business is different. Maybe that CEO only builds 15 houses per year. What if you build 500? How should you act? Just pick the top 10 per year. Start your ambassador work there.

What if your business sells to other businesses where customers only email you purchase orders based upon quotes? Then attend the closest meeting to your receipt of the purchase order.

What if you are a retailer or internet business who doesn't have in person launches and sells direct to clients in store? Find 10 events within the year where you can interact with your customers as an ambassador. Perhaps at an event you sponsor or an in-store launch.

The key is to not do other people's jobs, to be an ambassador at these events, and to prioritise the most important events for your organisation.

Story

It was around the 15th anniversary of Jake founding his business that I started working with him. He had built a successful mid-market business and, as a CEO, it was clear he was an engineer at heart.

Jake wasn't a sales person. He proudly claimed he was an engineer, and it almost felt he believed that selling was beneath him. Sure he had been involved in sales in the early days, but as soon as he could afford it he employed a sales person and didn't look back. When we started working together, Jake had 15 sales people and a sales manager. Jake firmly saw his job as running the business and overseeing the engineering and R&D teams, in truth the job he really enjoyed.

The problem was that Jake didn't really know his customers, and they certainly didn't know him. 'It's not what I'm good at,' he would say defensively, and he would go on to explain the job of the sales manager was to build relationships with clients. One day I challenged Jake around this and discussed the five roles of a CEO. In the other areas of Accountability, Culture, Strategy and Succession Planning he performed OK, but he was doing almost none of the Ambassador role.

After a while we agreed that Jake would start by attending the 10 major customer contract signings in the following year. It wasn't too much, and Jake agreed that it was achievable and was at least a start.

To his credit, a year later Jake had attended 11 contract signings and was comfortable in the role of ambassador at these meetings. He treated it as a gift to the client to say thank you, and he didn't try to be someone he wasn't. I encouraged him to let his love and pride for the technology and products shine through, something he was indeed comfortable with.

Then, after nine years with the business, the sales manager was head hunted by a competitor. Better salary, share options, new car, large bonus, the sales manager got everything that he wanted and more, but, his new employer wanted results. And that meant taking clients and sales people from Jake.

It took seven months for Jake to find a replacement sales manager he was happy with, and the former sales manager succeeded in taking three of Jake's best sales people in that time, placing enormous pressure on Jake who was the acting sales manager, CEO as well as head of engineering and R&D.

But thanks to the work we had done, Jake had built some basic relationships with clients. In his ambassadorial meetings his passion for the product had shone through and the clients could see it. During the seven months after the sales manager left, Jake met with all his major clients in an ambassadorial role and also built upon the relationships he had developed in the previous year, where he explained honestly the situation with the sales managers departure and Jake's unwavering commitment to the products.

Jake's new sales manager worked out well, and Jake continues to have Ambassador meetings on a regular basis, he has an understanding of the sales funnel and when larger contracts are due for signing he attends.

Tool

In the past year what have been the top 10 major product launches or contract signings for your business that you could have attended but didn't attend?

Looking to the year ahead, what are the top 10 major product launches or contract signings that are likely to occur that you could attend?

Finally attend as many as you can, be the Ambassador, don't try do anyone else's job and let your genuine love for the company and your products shine through.

Major product launches or contract signings you could have attended in the past year

DATE	PRODUCT LAUNCH OR CONTRACT SIGNING	EVENT

Major product launches or contract signings you may be able to attend in the next year

DATE	PRODUCT LAUNCH OR CONTRACT SIGNING	EVENT

Key points

★ Attending major product launches or customer signings in an ambassadorial role acknowledges the importance of these events.

★ This demonstrates that you care to customers and staff.

★ All businesses are different. Select appropriate events or meetings to attend given the size of your business.

Key Resources

★ *The 4-Hour Work Week: Escape the 9–5, Live Anywhere and Join the New Rich* - Tim Ferris

2.3 All employees learn Core Values and Core Purpose stories monthly from the CEO

Principle

If Core Values explain who the organisation is and the Core Purpose explains why the organisation exists, then who is accountable for everyone in the company both knowing and living the Core Values and Core Purpose?

A case may be made that all leaders throughout the organisation need to own the Core Values and Core Purpose and bring them to life, but ultimately the ownership for these must rest with the CEO in the role of Ambassador. If who your company is, and why you exist, is delegated to a line manager, or the human resources department, what will be the impact compared to a regular, rhythmic focus from the CEO?

You may be familiar with Carl W. Buehner's phrase, '*People may forget what you said but they will never forget how you made them feel*'. That statement resonates because our brains are hardwired to most effectively remember emotions and stories. And effective stories that make us feel something are the ones that we remember the most.

Think for a moment about a movie or TV show you easily remember. Think about what happened within the story and how that made you feel. Can you identify the emotions you experienced? It's likely you remember them because it made you feel something.

Our brains didn't evolve over tens of thousands of years to connect with spreadsheets or graphs, or even data retention in the form of acronyms. It was how a situation or person made you feel. It was a story about an event that happened.

That's why I'm very reluctant to have teams I work with build Core Values that are an acronym spelling out something in the hope team members will remember it, like R.E.C.I.P.E or D.R.I.V.E. The stories of genuine, lived behaviours within an organisation matter the most and will help people understand and remember the values that matter.

Once you have uncovered your Core Purpose and Core Values, and I would recommend between five and seven Core Values in total, you need to begin the process of bringing the Purpose and Values to life. The objective isn't to have these important statements about who you are and why you exist sitting on a plaque in your reception, gathering dust and having no one know what they are or what they mean. The objective is to create alignment within the team and create a tool to help leaders educate team members on the behavioural and cultural expectations of the company leadership.

One of the best ways to bring Core Values and Core Purpose to life is through stories. Stories about great things that have happened in the business recently, and whether these align with your Core Purpose or one of your Core Values. If someone really has done something great recently that showcased the definition of one of your Core Values or Purpose, who better than the CEO to acknowledge this great achievement.

Unless you're being mocked for the amount you talk about the Values and Purpose, you probably aren't talking about them enough as the CEO.

Story

When I started working with Tim, he said he had built Core Values that he felt were fine, and he didn't want to change them. A couple of years prior, he engaged an external consultant who conducted surveys and interviews with everyone in the business and looked for 'patterns', where the consultant then created six Values.

The problem was that two years later, at our first workshop, I realised that the Values not only weren't alive, but also weren't authentic. Furthermore, no one on the leadership team actually knew what they were.

I don't subscribe to the idea that the whole organisation should contribute to building the Core Values, and I never conduct Core Values discovery in that manner. First, in such a scenario, you are capturing the Values and behaviour of people who are not necessarily the type of employees you would like to emulate. Second, Core Values prescribe the type of behaviour that demonstrates who you are. These are the behavioural and cultural expectations that people should live by, as determined by the leaders. Therefore, when people don't live by these Values, it is up to the leaders to discipline people or coach people to understand why they aren't meeting the behavioural expectations. For that reason, it is primarily the shared Values of the leaders that should translate into the Core Values of the organisation.

It was very frustrating for Tim. He wanted Values that united his people and that he could use as an alignment tool with staff to praise and discipline. He had paid for it and undergone a discovery process, and yet the Core Values were not alive.

To Tim's credit, he decided to rebuild the Core Values from scratch. At our next workshop with the leadership team 90 days later, we set about building a new set of Core Values. Several months later, we had discovered the five new Core Values, and no matter how I tried, the team wouldn't change them, which is a simple test I use to validate their dedication. They were committed and believed that the new Core Values truly represented who they were. I like to say that the team who builds the plan doesn't fight the plan, and Tim's leadership team now had ownership over these Values as they had built them together.

When the time came to release the Core Values to other people in the business, we started with what I call guerrilla release tactics. That is, rather than having a big launch, the leadership team started having conversations about the Core Values with employees outside the leadership team.

On the down low. Just little chats here and there.

They mentioned during these chats that we had been working on Core Values and they were currently in draft format. Then they asked for an example of something great that someone had done recently. The leadership team member had to then connect the story about someone doing something great with a Core Value that we had built. The leadership team member would then discuss the other Core Values and stories that others had mentioned relating to each of the draft Core Values.

We validated the Values inside and outside the leadership team in an authentic and meaningful manner. Everyone felt a sense of ownership well before Tim had the formal launch. People knew that the Core Values were validated by great things that people had done in the business, and so after the launch, it was easy for Tim to continue the rhythm of Core Values stories connected to great things that people had done.

From there, Tim's team built Core Values and Core Purpose posters that told the best stories about the business.

Tool

First, you must consider the definition of a story.

A story is an account of real or imagined events or people. For example, *Jack and Jill went up the hill to fetch a pail of water. Jack fell down and broke his crown and Jill came tumbling after.*

This has a beginning – Jack and Jill going up the hill. It has a middle – Jack falling down and breaking his crown. It has an end – Jill tumbling after.

In order to create Core Values and Core Purpose stories, it is important to identify something great someone has done and then to capture it by understanding what the event was through its beginning, middle and end.

Over the years, I have documented hundreds upon hundreds of Core Values and Core Purpose stories during leadership team workshops. There can be a tendency for people to say something like, 'I am going to nominate Sarah for our Core Value of Tenacity because she is a hard worker and always gets her work done'. This is not a story and

Core Values / Core Purpose nomination form

Nominator name	*Your name*
Date	*Today's date*
Where	*The location and setting for the story*
What	*Which of our values or purpose does the story most relate to*
Who	*Who is the story about from our organisation*
Problem	*What was the problem*
Important events	*What were the key events that took place in the story*
Solution	*How was the problem resolved*

should be avoided at all costs. It doesn't describe an event, and it doesn't have a beginning, middle and end.

Also, you should not ask for a Core Values story directly. Instead ask for something great someone has done in the business recently. Then ask whether it connects with the Core Purpose, or if a Core Value, which Core Value.

Your system should involve collecting stories weekly or monthly depending on the size of your organisation, having them documented, having the leadership team elect the best of the best as an agenda item at weekly or monthly meetings and then having the CEO discuss the story of the month. This way the best stories rise to the top of the organisation.

The stories can be distributed in person, by email or video. Remember, though, this is an Ambassadorial role. An email written by an assistant or marketing person won't cut it. Distributing the stories in person is best. Via video is second best. Distribution by email is the least-preferred option.

From there you can build a quarterly or annual awards program for the best story of the quarter or year. You can also build a culture book containing stories or an internal company Wiki site where stories and photos are collected over time. For an example of Core Values stories, awards and a culture book from a team I work with, you can search the web for The Physio Co, who were recently named as one of Australia's Best Places to Work for the tenth year in a row. Remember the key is for the CEO to be recognising great achievements that align with the Values or Purpose.

Above is an example form to use for collecting Core Values stories. It breaks down the event so it is easily translatable into a story, as well as being easy to complete.

Key points

* ★ The human brain has evolved to recall stories and recall the way something makes you feel.
* ★ Core Values and Core Purpose are brought alive through stories about great things people have done, and how these connect with the Core Values or Core Purpose.
* ★ As an ambassador for the company Core Values and Core Purpose, employees should learn these great stories from the leader.

Key Resources

* ★ *Richard Evans' Quote Book* - Richard L. Evans

2.4 All new employees are welcomed by the CEO either physically or virtually within their first week of employment

Principle

In small businesses recruitment, typically the owner or CEO interviews every candidate and makes the decision to hire. Meanwhile, the candidate develops an understanding of what type of leader they are enlisting with.

As an organisation grows, the CEO becomes less involved in hiring. The task is often taken up by department managers and recruiting professionals. So how do new employees learn about their CEO, the person who they have entrusted this stage of their career and reputation to?

Unfortunately it's often gossip, internet research and limited, uncontrolled interactions, such as passing in the hall or in the elevator. This isn't a reliable system to create a positive first impression! As the CEO, you need to be out there as the Ambassador, interacting with your employees and new hires.

The influence and interactions with the CEO are important because power does not depend only on the leader; power depends also on the perceptions that the followers have of the leader.

And perceptions are shaped by the experience a person has.

When a person joins a new company, they are also joining the potential positive impact that company can have on their career and personal situation. They're excited! No one joins a company thinking they will be disappointed in their new job. People aren't thinking that they are definitely going to be let down.

No, it's the leaders in the business that do that.

As Marcus Buckingham writes in his book, *First, Break All the Rules: What the World's Greatest Managers Do Differently*, 'People leave managers not companies'. That's because the company hasn't let them down – the managers have.

In the first week of employment, new hires should have a positive experience from four different perspectives that align with the four prides of a team detailed in the Culture chapter of this book.

PRODUCT - The new hire should experience a positive introduction to the product or service you sell. Why are you proud of the product or service you sell? Is it price, volume, quality, design? The new hire should be absolutely clear on why you and your team are proud of your product.

MANAGER - The new hire should experience a positive and supportive interaction with their manager. The manager should ideally outline every aspect of the expectations the manager has for the role to the point it isn't possible for them to misunderstand, and to build a 90-day onboarding plan – everything the new hire must achieve and understand in the first 90 days.

TEAM - The new hire should experience a positive and supportive interaction with their teammates. This should include a formal induction process which has the new hire spend time with several different people walking them through processes, as well as perhaps a welcome party. As the legendary sales coach Jack Daly says, why do we give people a party when they resign, are fed up with our company and are off to work for our competition? We need to throw a party when they arrive, not when they go!

COMPANY - The new hire should be welcomed and learn about the company from the CEO acting in an ambassadorial role. This should reinforce the message from the manager and team, discussing Core Values and Purpose as well as the vision for the company. Importantly it's about them and not you. Do you love playing polo on weekends or racing cars? Save it for another time. Outline why the company exists, why it matters and why the new hire is an important part of that mission.

Story

Helen was a hyper busy CEO. Often when we would meet she would cut our meetings short and have other meetings backing up. She felt that she was more effective by taking on more. In fact, the more she took on, the more effective she felt. Helen also believed that her leadership team should be busy and their interactions seemed to involve Helen creating an ongoing stream of new ideas and activities for all to commence.

It always felt like Helen didn't have clarity. It felt like she was busy, but not effective. This isn't unique to Helen. Many CEOs I work with exhibit similar behaviours. One of our goals is to get the CEO in control, and to have the CEO, and to a lesser degree the leadership team, as the least busy people in the business. In good businesses, the leadership team are the busiest. In great businesses, the leadership team are the least busy.

Helen had just over 100 employees and was by all accounts very successful, but she was so busy that almost all of the time she spent with employees was spent with the leadership team. For her, recruiting and onboarding was the responsibility of managers, and she only wanted to know that vacant roles were filled with good people.

At a meeting one day the subject of an employee's recent resignation was being discussed, a person who had only been at the business for nine months. This piqued Helen's interest as she felt a pattern was emerging, that the new hire retention was not good. Helen's hunch seemed to be correct as a subsequent analysis of the data revealed that of the 27 people who were hired in the past year, 12 had resigned.

When we analysed the data further, we learned that the price of this problem was in fact enormous and had cost the organisation between $950k and $1.1m in the past year. This was a relatively conservative estimate and included recruitment fees, advertising, training, lost productivity and profit from lost sales. It didn't consider employee morale or employee brand damage.

Helen was shocked. She wondered what the managers were doing to these good people to make them leave so early. She wondered why managers were not supporting the staff in their new role.

Let's just say that she didn't warmly embrace my analogy that the fish rots from the head down, and that leadership is the root cause of an organisation's failure and demise. But she accepted the challenge, and accepted that she was at least partly responsible.

My question to her was simple: how much time, not money, would you be prepared to dedicate on an ongoing basis each and every month to solve this issue?

After some discussion, we agreed that 1% of her time per month dedicated to new employees was suitable. So we set about formally involving her in the onboarding process, knowing that we could not allocate more than two hours per month to new employees, and that the time Helen spent had to have maximum impact for new employees.

At first, we had Helen spend an hour with new employees on their first or second day. Each month there was one or two new hires, so it wasn't overwhelming. We developed key talking points to address and agreed that Helen couldn't take her phone or tablet into the meeting to prevent distraction. She could only talk about her passion and her vision for the company.

That action along with other initiatives to improve new hire retention resulted in 31 hires and only 6 departures the next year.

Helen recognised the need for her to perform the role of Ambassador and now looks forward to sharing her passion and vision with new recruits.

Tool

Spending ambassadorial time with new employees isn't difficult, but it is highly impactful to new employees. In fact it's probably one of the highest impacting one-on-one things you can do with your time.

Clearly it depends on the size of your business. If you have 100 employees with 20% new hires each year, this would represent just over four meetings per month. If you have 40,000 employees with 6% new hires per year, that's 46 new employees per week.

Like Helen, perhaps start with a time commitment. Truthfully, 1% or two hours per month isn't onerous. But given the size and geographic

Sample welcome from CEO agenda

AGENDA ITEM	KEY POINTS THIS MONTH FOR THE COMPANY	KEY POINTS FOR THIS PERSONS DEPARTMENT
Welcome	Overview of this months cohort	
Our values	Recent Core Values story	Recent Core Values story from this department
Our purpose	Recent Core Purpose story	Recent Core Purpose story from this department
Our BHAG®	Progress toward BHAG®	How your department contributes to our BHAG®
Our strategy	Progress on our strategy	How your department contributes to our strategy
Annual priorities	Annual company priorities and progress	Department priorities and progress
Quarterly priorities	Quarterly priorities and what the company is focussed on right now	Department quarterly priorities
Your role	How your role fits into the bigger picture of the company	How your role fits into the department
Q&A		

spread of your organisation, how can you make the two hours count for the most?

If you search online, you will find many examples of employee welcome videos, which are great, but that's not what I'm suggesting. Those videos are not timely and often feel like a marketing pitch.

If your organisation has 40,000 employees I'm not suggesting you read out all 46 names, but figure a way to personalise a video or webinar for that cohort, and do one every month! For example, '*I know in this August 2018 cohort we have 30 new staff joining us in Mumbai under the guidance of Manesh and another 7 in London under Paul*'.

Of course, if you only have 50 staff there may be no point in recording videos. Simply meeting or video conferencing with them may suffice. But whether you meet in person, remotely or record a video, you will need an agenda.

A sample welcome from the CEO agenda is outlined on the previous page.

Key points

★ Leaders in mid-sized firms can often have little interaction with new hires; therefore, new hires risk learning about the CEO via inappropriate, and often inaccurate methods.

★ New hires should have a positive experience with the product, manager, team and company in their first week.

★ A positive welcome from the leader, in an appropriate form is a key part of this.

Key Resources

★ *First, Break All the Rules: What the World's Greatest Managers Do Differently* - Marcus Buckingham

2.5 Every quarter the CEO launches the company plan and priorities to all employees

Principle

In research for their book *The Leadership Challenge* James Kouzes and Barry Posner found that people are mostly motivated not by fear or reward, but by ideas that capture their imagination.

The fact that organisations had a vision mattered much less than communicating them effectively. The great leaders identified by Kouzes and Posner were future-oriented and endeavoured to bring people along by energising them with passion, enthusiasm and emotion.

These leaders undertook two primary activities to align people. First, they envisioned an uplifting and ennobling future that inspired team members. Second, they enlisted others in their vision by appealing to their values, interests, hopes and dreams.

Many other researchers have come to similar conclusions – that high-performing leaders effectively communicate their vision, which then motivates and aligns team members to all work on the right priorities.

In the 2009 book *Predictable Results In Unpredictable Times*, Stephen Covey and Bob Whitman identified that only 15% of employees knew their company's top priorities. Even worse, only 6% know their own individual priorities.

For middle managers, Donald Sull, Rebecca Homkes and Charles Sull found in their HBR article "Why strategy execution unravels and what to do about it", that only 55% of middle managers can name even one of their company's top five priorities.

Let's consider that for a moment. Most people are not working on the top priorities their company must execute. Even worse, most people don't even know what those priorities are.

The result?

According to Harvard Business School, 90% of strategies fail due to poor execution.

As if that isn't bad enough, consider the effect on employee engagement.

Without a compelling vision for the organisation and priorities that are shared and measured with momentum to drive their successful execution, top performers are not attracted and often times repelled, whereas people who are seeking 'just a job' are getting exactly what they want.

To increase the successful execution of your strategy and improve employee engagement, you must undertake the Ambassadorial role to launch the plan and priorities. You must communicate the vision in a manner that motivates and aligns all employees to feel a sense of ownership over the result.

Story

I'd been working with Steve for around a year, and he was getting frustrated with the poor execution of priorities by his leadership team. Each quarter, when we left our quarterly planning workshops, the leadership team agreed that these were the most important priorities. Yet once they went back to their day-to-day job, somehow the days and weeks passed, and very little action was taken to execute these priorities. Then we would get to the end of the quarter, when the priorities were due to be completed and very few would be finished.

I asked them what they thought was causing poor execution of these priorities, and their reply was something to the effect that I didn't understand how busy they were, and that things were different there.

As much as the leaders were not doing what they said they would, Steve was equally responsible because he was not being an Ambassador in bringing the plan and priorities to life. As the saying goes 'people respect what you inspect' and Steve was only paying attention to the priorities when they were set and when they were due.

He was subliminally sending a message to his leadership team that he didn't really care that much about the successful execution of the priorities.

His frustration was clear. 'But why don't they just do their job, what I pay them for?' he asked, seeming confused. 'Because they are human and not machines, because humans experience emotions and need motivation and direction', I replied. We worked through Steve's role as an Ambassador in owning and launching the plan and priorities that day and developed a simple framework to launch these after each quarterly offsite planning workshop.

It's not that Steve didn't want to undertake the Ambassador role in this context, he just didn't know that he had to. The tool we built is detailed below, and Steve used it to launch the next quarterly plan and priorities and improved his teams priority execution from an average of 36% to 75% with each iteration over the coming year.

Tool

The outcome of a successful launch is having team members know the company plan and priorities. The outcome of a leadership team offsite workshop is a series of priorities for the company and for each department. These priorities are the 'what'. What the leadership team will achieve. The thing that hasn't yet been determined is 'how'. How the leadership team members will achieve the 'what'.

That's what the first week after a leadership team offsite day is used for. It enables leadership team members to validate their assumptions from the quarterly workshop and to build a detailed plan explaining *how* they will achieve the *what* (the priorities). At the first weekly meeting the team should stress test each other's plans on how they will achieve the 3-5 priorities for their department.

Then as soon as possible afterward, ideally the following day, the CEO launches the plan and priorities to the whole company for the quarter. This should include posters and dashboards to measure the progress as appropriate to suit the size of your organisation. Remember this can be as simple as writing on a whiteboard or flipchart paper or as complex as you like.

What is important is that the CEO, in the Ambassador role, has launched the plan and priorities, explaining why each is important and how each connects to the broader vision of the organisation. Maybe your company is too large, and you would need to launch in different regions or by video or webinar. But the task remains to clearly explain the plan and priorities to all employees in such a manner so that they clearly understand it.

Company Plan Launch Planner

	LEADERSHIP TEAM OFFSITE DATE	FIRST WEEKLY MEETING DATE	LAUNCH DATE	MONTHLY MEETING DATES	WEEKLY MEETING DATES
Purpose	Set company and department priorities	Leadership team members present detailed plans on how they will execute their priorities in the coming quarter	CEO launches the plans and priorities at a company wide meeting with dashboards and posters	Major analysis of priority progress	Minor analysis of priority progress
Example	14th June	21st June	22nd June	10am, 2nd Wednesday of the month	Wednesday 10am
Q1					
Q2					
Q3					
Q4					

Key points

★ High-performing leaders effectively communicate their vision, which then motivates and aligns team members to all work on the right priorities.

★ Most people are not working on the top priorities their company must execute. Even worse, most people don't even know what those priorities are.

★ In the role of Ambassador a leader must communicate the vision in a manner that motivates and aligns all employees to feel a sense of ownership over the result.

Key Resources

★ *The Leadership Challenge* - James Kouzes and Barry Posner

★ *Predictable Results In Unpredictable Times* - Stephen Covey and Bob Whitman

★ "Why strategy execution unravels and what to do about it" - Harvard Business Review - Donald Sull, Rebecca Homkes and Charles Sull

★ CULTURE

3.0 A positive culture unites the team and attracts the right people

What is culture and why do so many leaders find it challenging?

In a 2018 Egon Zehnder survey of 402 CEOs from 11 countries, the survey's author states '68% of CEOs admitted they didn't feel fully prepared for the job'. He went on: 'CEOs told us that while they did feel ready for the strategic and business aspects of their roles, they felt much less prepared for the personal and interpersonal components of leadership, which are just as critical to success'.

The problem when building a positive culture is that not only do CEOs find the cultural and ideological aspects of their position challenging, but the general public is sceptical about the motives of CEOs. The 2018 Edelman Trust Barometer showed 60% of respondents believed that CEOs were more driven by greed than a desire to make a positive difference in the world. Interestingly, the same survey outlined that 56% believed the companies that only thought about themselves and their profits were bound to fail.

To surmise, more people than not think that CEOs care mostly about their own personal benefit, and those CEOs who don't care are bound to fail.

If we look back to the origins of the word culture, we see it is derived from the Latin word '*colere*,' which means to care or to cultivate.

In the context of your role as a CEO, when it comes to culture, your job is to care for, or cultivate your people.

As Teddy Roosevelt said, 'No one cares how much you know, until they know how much you care'.

To cultivate your people and build a positive culture, people need to know how much you care.

Imagine you are the custodian of each person you employ. Eventually every person will leave to get another job. So that means each person has a beginning, a middle and an end with you. As their custodian, how are you cultivating your people during this time? How are you caring for them? After the end, will they look back on their time under your custodianship as good, bad or great?

Even if you had to fire someone, did you do the right thing by them? Did you care and cultivate them through a difficult time?

Think about the people who have left your employ. Could you phone them up today and have a good conversation? Or have you left a trail of destruction, like the U.S. Shark Tank TV show judge Kevin O'Leary, who, when he doesn't get the deal, says 'You're dead to me!' Even worse, is your legacy a series of lawsuits?

I don't by any means proclaim you should be a pushover. Remember this caring and cultivating of the people in your custody also occurs within the context of your first role of Accountability, holding people accountable with consequences in a disciplined environment.

According to Dr. Gerald Bell of Bell Leadership, being proud as an employee is a human need that must be fulfilled.

Employees must be:

★ Proud of their product
★ Proud of their manager
★ Proud of their team
★ Proud of their company

Or they will eventually leave.

To care for your people, to cultivate them and to get the most from them, is to understand their natural need to be proud.

If you are supporting a manager who isn't making people around them proud, the message you are sending to all is that you don't really care enough to make the difficult choice of exiting, or training, or reprimanding that manager. That message you send, like it or not, is received by people wanting to find a leader who does care enough.

But while caring and cultivating employees during your time together is one important factor, the four prides identified above are dependant on integrity, and the problem is that many companies, teams, bosses or products don't live up to the promises they make.

Have you seen the memes showing a comparison between the hamburger on a TV advertisement to the hamburger a customer received? What about insurance that doesn't meet its intent or banks that cheat customers? Those failures impact the integrity of the product, and the pride of the employees.

The same can be said for bosses, teams and companies. Every time you don't live up to a promise you made to an employee, you are indirectly impacting your productivity and retention rate.

The culture of the business is consciously or unconsciously prescribed by the CEO and the efficacy of that prescription occurs based upon the capability of the CEOs leadership and personal skills.

As the diagram below adapted from Dr. Bell demonstrates, for a worker to succeed, they will require 80% technical skills and only 20% leadership and personality skills. Whereas for a CEO to succeed, they will only require 20% technical skills but 80% leadership and personality skills.

The further you rise in an organisation, the more you depend on leadership and personality skills to succeed.

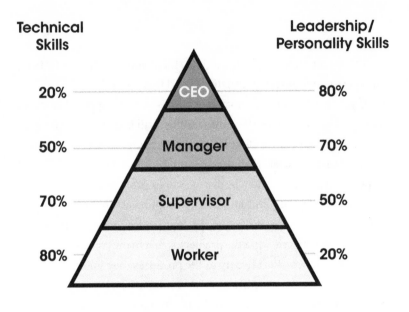

Technical Skills — Leadership/Personality Skills

- CEO: 20% / 80%
- Manager: 50% / 70%
- Supervisor: 70% / 50%
- Worker: 80% / 20%

In thinking about your role, consider not only the importance of your leadership and personality skills, but also those people you support, your managers and supervisors whose success in their role is dependant at least 50% on their leadership and personality skills.

To have a positive culture that unites the team and attracts the right people is to have all people cared for and being cultivated.

Key points

- ★ Look at the origin of the word culture: it means to care for or cultivate.
- ★ As a leader, your role relating to culture is to care for and cultivate people during their tenure with you.
- ★ Employees must be proud of their product, manager, team and company, or they will eventually leave.
- ★ The further you rise in an organisation, the more you depend on leadership and personality skills to succeed.

Key Resources

- ★ Egon Zehnder survey - https://www.egonzehnder.com/ceo-study-2018/highlights
- ★ Edelman Trust Barometer 2018 - https://www.edelman.com/trust-barometer
- ★ Dr Gerald Bell - Bell Leadership Institute

3.1 Core Values and Core Purpose are known by all employees

Principle

In their book *Built to Last: Successful Habits of Visionary Companies*, Jim Collins and Jerry Porras, explain the importance of profit to a company.

'Profitability is a necessary condition for the existence and a means to more important ends, but it is not the end in itself for many of the visionary companies,' he writes. 'Profit is like oxygen, food, water, and blood for the body; they are not the point of life, but without them, there is no life.'

It doesn't matter if you are the CEO of a privately-owned business, a publicly listed company, a charitable non-profit or a Government department, you must pursue both the vision and purpose of the organisation as well as ensure the organisation has sufficient profitability. For the most powerful Core Values, or the most noble purposes in the world are not even worth considering if you can't pay your bills and ultimately close the doors.

Some organisations are completely focussed on maximising profitability, are frugal in everything they do and spend little effort on their people, the long-term vision or purpose of the organisation.

Other organisations build a people-centred organisation with customer and staff happiness as their focus and an altruistic vision and purpose, yet neglect their budget and profit targets, thereby depriving the organisation of the vitality to live up to its potential.

A leader who aims to thrive must ensure a balance between both profitability and people.

If the organisation is not consistently performing at an acceptable profitability level, it will not survive and will be incapable of living its purpose and achieving its vision.

Equally, if the organisation is not able to connect its people to a broader vision and purpose, it will not be able to maximise the potential of its people and assets into the future.

According to The Deloitte Millennial Survey 2018, a survey of more than 12,000 Millennial and Gen-Z respondents across 36 countries, only 24% of Millennials believed their employers objectives *should* be generating profits. However, 51% said their employers actual objectives *were* generating profits, highlighting a disconnect in culture between what Millennials value and what they see their companies actually doing. Millennials think their employers need to be about both profit and purpose, working from a socially conscious perspective. Be aware of that cultural desire. Remember that profit can't be everything.

In responding to this viewpoint, you should assume that respondents generally don't understand accounting or the realities of business profitability. In a 2013 Reason-Rupe poll, respondents said they believed that the average manufacturing company makes 34% profit after taxes. Furthermore, the average respondent believes that a reasonable profit after taxes was 36%. This is an enormous difference to reality where a 2018 NYU Stern analysis of profit margin by sector, conducted by Professor Aswath Damodaran reports a median industry net profit margin of just 6%.

If you own a business with $10 million in revenues, the average person believes you are making a $3.4 million profit after taxes, whereas it is more likely you are making closer to $600,000 after taxes if you compare with the average industry profit margin. Whether or not you share financial results with your staff is a personal decision, but knowing the misconceptions the average person has about profit is fundamentally important to understanding their decision-making process and their motivations.

You cannot alter the beliefs of millennials, and you may not want to educate your staff on the realities of corporate profitability, but you can help your staff understand the Core Values and the Core Purpose of your organisation. Indeed having people understand the values that are most important and why the organisation exists is something you have complete control over.

At a team meeting one afternoon when researching the book *Built to Last* one of Jim Collins research assistants made a comment about the visionary companies that were the best in their industry, 'Joining these companies reminds me of joining an extremely tight knit group or society. And if you don't fit you'd better not join. If you're willing to really buy in and dedicate yourself to what the company stands for, then you'll be very satisfied and productive - probably couldn't be happier. If not, however, you'll probably flounder, feel miserable, and out of place, and eventually leave - ejected like a virus. It's binary: you're either in or you're out, and there seems to be no middle ground. It's almost cult like'.

The three cultural attributes that separated the 'Built to Last' visionary companies were:

★ Stronger indoctrination into a core ideology
★ Greater tightness of fit - people tend to fit well into the company and its ideology or not fit at all
★ Greater elitism - a sense of belonging to something special and superior

In summary, the visionary companies showed greater cultism.

The job of the CEO is to most effectively harness peoples energy and desire by building a closely aligned team, with shared purpose and values, along with a belief in achieving a common vision.

Therefore, to positively impact productivity and retention on your team, employees must deeply understand the Core Values and Core Purpose, to the degree that people who don't fit are ejected like a virus.

In the context of your cultural norms, how can you make your culture a little more cultish?

Story

As a business owner with a degree in mathematics, one might suspect that Michael Malone's attention would be drawn more toward the numbers and the engineering rather than customer service.

When Malone founded his business in 1993 he had just graduated from the University of Western Australia and was about to lose his access to the internet, and the community of bulletin boards and information sharing he had come to love. Back then the internet wasn't what it is today with instant web browsers, images and video, the internet consisted of computers within university and research campuses connecting to one another, exchanging lines of code via modems. There simply were no internet service providers to buy access from outside of these institutions.

Says Malone, 'I looked at the cost of getting my own link to the US, just for me. That was about $25,000 a year and that was well beyond my reach. So, I asked some other university students if I set something up and started offering it commercially, would you be willing to buy it?'

To make it work he needed 200 people to give him $25 per month to cover costs and turn his hobby into a business, thereby creating Western Australia's first internet provider offering 14kB dial up internet access to the public. So, he put together the $25,000 with a loan from his parents and established iiNet.

A year later and Malone had successfully secured the 200 paid subscribers he needed when Netscape launched the first web browser, making it easy for the general public to use the internet, and in the next three months he signed up another 1,000 customers.

This period of rapid growth was challenging, and he quickly learnt that if the technology was set up and engineered correctly, it generally worked. It was the customers who were both the challenge, and the opportunity. This is where the strategy for iiNet was first established, as he describes it to 'lead on product, differentiate on customer service'. In order to capture and maintain market share, iiNet was going to focus on delivering the best customer service in the industry, an industry with a reputation for the technician on a call perhaps being passionate about computers, but likely not being passionate about customer service.

Says Malone, 'One of our staff had worked in five-star hotels and told us we should be hiring people in the hospitality industry. He ended up becoming our first customer-service manager'.

The big challenge was bringing on enough people with the technical ability and the potential to provide great customer service to match the growth of iiNet. That meant hiring for attitude and indoctrinating people into the iiNet culture through an immersive onboarding.

In the early 2000s, a key part of this onboarding was Michael Malone jumping in his car with the new recruits and driving them from the city office to his parent's garage in the Perth suburb of Padbury where the company originated. During the trip Malone would explain the values and purpose of the company, and why customer service was so important at iiNet. He would show them the rooms that housed dozens of modems where as a start-up he would take calls and delight customers.

New recruits would leave this tour with a deep understanding of the values, purpose and culture of the organisation, and in the critical early stages, every person in the company knew who the team was and the importance of customer service.

People were being indoctrinated into the tight knit group that was iiNet. They were buying in to the culture that was dedicated to providing the best customer service, and Michael Malone as CEO was ensuring that everyone understood the values and purpose. New recruits had a choice, they bought into the cultish iiNet culture, or they self-selected if they felt they didn't fit.

In 2007 iiNet was one of the first Telco companies in the world to adopt Net Promoter Score, a measure of customer satisfaction, and to connect the bonuses of employees to their NPS result. By 2012, iiNet had the highest NPS score of all DSL Internet Services Providers globally with a +56.7 NPS, while the number two was France's Free with a +18 NPS. There wasn't an Australian DSL competitor with an NPS above 0. Also, in 2013 iiNet had calculated that every percent increase (i.e. from +56 to +57) had a $1.65m measurable positive impact on the company.

By 2014 iiNet had 1 million broadband customers, a market cap of $1.23 billion, was the number-one DSL broadband provider globally by NPS, and number two in Australia by market share.

Having everyone in the business understand the Core Values and Core Purpose at iiNet, which were integral to the culture they needed to build, enabled the iiNet team to scale with the right people.

Tool

In the table below, consider the options to ensure all employees know your Core Values and Core Purpose. The objective should not be to have people simply recite them, but for them to be alive, to make it simply not possible for people to misunderstand what they are and the intent behind them.

You should only consider actions you are comfortable with and ideas that feel appropriate to your culture. However, as you decide, be conscious that what you are trying to do is to make your culture a little more cultish, to not only make your values and purpose known, but by being clear on the things your people value, and why you exist, you are helping those who don't belong to self-select out.

Worth doing? Yes or no? Begin by considering whether the idea is suitable in your situation, whether it is a cultural norm and you are comfortable doing it. In the worth doing column place a yes or no.

Who can own it? Next, if you listed yes for the idea being worth doing, who in your organisation can own it? Who would bring energy and enthusiasm to a project like this and feel rewarded by it's completion?

Expand the idea. Get some initial ideas about how to best make this concept work in your organisation. For example, for posters, the first idea, you may want to develop posters with the best stories about how employees have lived your Core Purpose and post them around your workplace.

When we should complete. Finally list when you can complete it. Don't plan to complete everything in the next 90 days. I find it's better to really think about the order you want to roll the ideas out and then begin one idea after you have finished the last idea in a sequential order to not only avoid overwhelming the employees implementing the ideas, but to have the overall team able to accept one new idea at a time. Execute one thing well and then move onto the next.

Other ideas. While there are ten ideas below, consider what other ideas you can use to bring values and purpose to life in your organisation.

Ideas to bring values and purpose to life

	WORTH DOING YES / NO	WHO CAN OWN IT	EXPAND THE IDEA	WHEN WE SHOULD COMPLETE
Posters				
Awards				
Dashboards / Screensavers				
Agenda in meetings for stories				
Merchandise				
Games				
Mascots				
Culture book				
Website / jobs page				
Recruitment & onboarding				
OTHER IDEAS				

Key points

★ In order to build a thriving business leaders must ensure a balance between both profitability and people.

★ The average person believes that the average company makes 34% profit after taxes, yet the average company actually makes closer to 6% profit after taxes.

★ Many employees believe their employers objectives should be about profits and purpose, yet observe only profit objectives.

★ Great, sustainable companies demonstrate greater cultism, with strong Core Values and Core Purpose part of a culture that seemingly ejects those who don't buy in.

Key Resources

★ *Built to Last: Successful Habits of Visionary Companies* - Jim Collins and Jerry I. Porras

★ The Deloitte Millennial Survey 2018 - https://www2.deloitte.com/global/en/pages/about-deloitte/articles/millennialsurvey

★ 2013 Reason-Rupe poll - https://www.scribd.com/document/166175880/Reason-Rupe-Poll-May-2013-Toplines

★ NYU Stern, Profit margin by sector - http://pages.stern.nyu.edu/~adamodar/New_Home_Page/datafile/margin.html

★ iiNET NPS - http://www.iinet.net.au/about/mediacentre/releases/07-08-2013-record-high-customer-satisfaction-gives-iinet-plenty-to-celebrate.pdf

3.2 There is a qualitative and quantitative system of feedback between all employees and leaders

Principle

In the 2014 HBR article, 'Your employees want the negative feedback you hate to give', Jack Zegner and Joseph Folkman outlined their research on people providing and receiving positive and negative feedback. For the purpose of the study, positive feedback included praise, reinforcement and congratulatory comments, whereas potentially negative feedback such as suggestions for improvement, explorations of new and better ways to do things, or pointing out something that was done in a less that optimal way was classified as corrective feedback.

In the chart below, adapted from this HBR article, the first column demonstrates that approximately the same number of people prefer to give positive feedback as those who do not.

The second column indicates that people are much more likely to prefer receiving positive feedback compared to giving positive feedback (column 1).

The third column shows how much people prefer to avoid giving negative feedback and that it is interestingly to the same degree that people prefer to receive positive feedback.

GIVING AND RECEIVING FEEDBACK

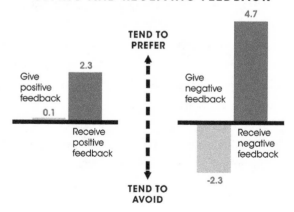

Finally, column four shows that people are roughly three times more likely to prefer receiving negative feedback than they are to avoid giving negative feedback.

Why did people want negative feedback? Overall, 72% of respondents said they thought their performance would improve if their managers would provide corrective feedback.

To summarise, people are twice as likely to prefer receiving negative feedback compared to receiving positive feedback but, people are three times more likely to avoid giving negative feedback.

No one likes to give negative feedback, but everyone wants to hear it.

Because people are more likely to avoid giving negative feedback, yet receiving it is so important to recipients, you should consider the development of a system to ensure this critical component of people development is maintained over time.

This system should be both quantitative to provide leaders with data to enable trends to be monitored and the right questions asked about data changes, and qualitative to obtain information that is relative to your current company situation.

In his book *The Ideal Team Player: How to Recognize and Cultivate The Three Essential Virtues*, Patrick Lencioni identifies the three root causes of job misery:

★ **ANONYMITY** - If you don't feel known by your manager, you won't love your job.
★ **IRRELEVANCE** - Everyone needs to know their job matters to someone. Anyone.
★ **IMMEASUREMENT** – People need to get tangible feedback which isn't based on the opinions of others.

The system of feedback you create should address these three root causes of job misery:

- ★ **ANONYMITY** – It should include one-on-one conversations between an employee and their manager.
- ★ **IRRELEVANCE** – It should make employees aware that their job matters to both their manager and other leaders.
- ★ **IMMEASUREMENT** – As well as qualitative feedback it should include quantitative data that both employee and manager are unable to dispute.

Finally, the system should consistently utilise a mix of both positive and corrective feedback, and be structured at regular intervals such as monthly or quarterly.

The four components of the system are outlined below:

1. QUALITATIVE FEEDBACK FROM MANAGERS

In the tool for this section below you will find a template you can provide to managers to provide the positive feedback and corrective feedback from a manager to an employee.

2. QUANTITATIVE FEEDBACK FROM MANAGERS

What data do you have, or can you develop, that clearly demonstrates the performance of the employee, their role or their department that is indisputable?

Pat Lencioni says that salespeople are some of the happiest employees because they are always acutely aware of their performance.

When a sportsperson isn't performing at the desired level their coach spends very little time explaining the consequence that they will be cut from the team and a great deal of time coaching to improve performance. With this data, employees should be acutely aware of any difference between actual and expected performance, but, like the sports coach, a great deal of the managers time should be spent on how the employee can achieve the desired results.

3. QUALITATIVE FEEDBACK FROM EMPLOYEES

The job of a manager is to get the most out of the people they support, their direct reports.

In her book *Multipliers: How the Best Leaders Make Everyone Smarter,* Liz Wiseman found that the best managers, who she described as 'Multipliers', get twice the capability from their direct reports compared to the 'Diminishers', the managers who shut down the smarts of their direct reports.

Therefore, if the job of a manager is to get the most from their direct reports, it is crucial that the manager obtains feedback, both positive and corrective from their direct reports about their performance as a manager, to ensure they are accessing people's capabilities, and not shutting down their smarts. See the tool at the end of this section for sample questions.

4. QUANTITATIVE FEEDBACK FROM EMPLOYEES

What is the data from employees that leaders cannot dispute, that when monitored over time will help leaders to ask the right questions and make the right decisions?

For example, how happy are the employees in our Sydney office compared to our Singapore office, and how has that changed in the past year? How has employee satisfaction changed since our merger? Or which of our offices has the lowest employee satisfaction?

Without this statistically repeatable data that you can rely on about employees, you will not be able to ask the right questions that lead to answers that let your leadership team make the right decisions.

There are several tools you can use for this such as Employee Net Promoter Score (eNPS), Tiny Pulse, Culture Amp and 15Five.

The key here is to develop a system that you can rely on. One of the ways to ensure this is to make the data from these manager interactions an agenda item on your monthly leadership team meeting, and have a leadership team person accountable to report the qualitative and quantitative data to the leadership team.

Story

I met Dan a few years ago, but I'm always reminded of his story when I think about employee engagement. Dan was a technician at a System Integrator, a company that installs computer and telephone systems, and from everything I could gather he was a pretty good employee. He seemed to manage sizable projects and deliver those projects without issues.

Dan was approaching his second anniversary at the company when he was managing a large telephone project for a utility customer. The plan was to change from the old telephone system to the new system over a weekend, something that Dan had done many times before and was completely familiar with.

Around 9.30 a.m. on Saturday morning Dan made a horrible discovery. One of the key parts for the system was missing, and that meant the installation could not be completed. To make matters worse the old system had already been removed and disconnected, and it wasn't possible to turn back. It was just at that moment, when Dan was struck with the realisation that no matter how many times he looked through the delivery boxes, that the critical part wasn't on site, when Andrea, the customer, arrived to check Dan's progress. Being aware of the project plan, Andrea enquired about the new system not being installed as yet, and Dan felt it only appropriate to share that he had just realised he was missing the part. Andrea, who was paying Dan's company to install the system, was acutely aware of the risk to her own job if her company didn't have operating telephones on Monday and was straight on the phone to Dan's boss Phil, who didn't answer. She left an angry voicemail message.

After around an hour of panic, Dan rang a friend who worked for a competitor of his company and managed to 'loan' a part from their stock and get the system working. By Sunday lunch time Dan still hadn't heard from his boss Phil, but he had finished the project and went home to enjoy the final hours of his weekend.

Phil was a laid back manager, some might say too laid back. He believed he was effective because he let people get on with their job, and that meant he wasn't a micro-manager. But the reality was that he was so busy he barely had the time to talk with his own people. Dan explained to me how the next day Phil barely mentioned the call from Andrea, their first interaction about the potentially disastrous mistake, and how he wasn't necessarily expecting praise for saving the project or to be yelled at because of the original mistake, but certainly expected some interaction. The fact that Phil barely acknowledged that something happened made Dan feel unimportant. As he put it, 'It's silly but I feel a bit like a kid looking for any attention, positive or negative from their parents. Anything would have been better than nothing. I just didn't know how Phil felt about the situation.'

About six months later, Dan had left his job and moved to another company. I asked him what was it that made him leave and why did he choose that particular new employer? He explained that during the interview for the new role, the boss left the room and he was able to chat with employees who would later become his colleagues. During that time he asked what it was like to work for their boss, and the response was that you always know where you stand. Positive or negative, you always know how the boss feels about your performance. Dan said sitting in that boardroom as he reflected on what they said, he realised that in the two and a half years he had worked with Phil he couldn't remember one time Phil provided him any form of meaningful feedback.

Tool

Some managers will provide regular feedback to their staff, and others will provide almost none. The intention of this tool is to use a system that provides a consistent level of feedback. You can use it monthly or quarterly – all that matters is that you do it consistently.

In a one-on-one meeting, the first four questions are posed and the manager's response documented. The second four questions are for the employee, and their response is also documented.

This should remain a conversation, and you should resist the urge to have people simply complete a form as the direct and contextual feedback and the opportunity for clarifying questions is important.

One on One Feedback Tool

MANAGER QUESTION | **MANAGER RESPONSE**

MANAGER QUESTION	MANAGER RESPONSE
Q1 Name something that the employee has done recently that has either impressed or pleased the manager?	
Q2 Describe one area the employee could improve or become more effective?	
Q3 What one thing could the employee stop doing to become more effective?	
Q4 What should the employee continue doing that they are doing well?	

MANAGER QUESTION | **EMPLOYEE RESPONSE**

MANAGER QUESTION	EMPLOYEE RESPONSE
Q5 What one thing does the manager do well when dealing with the employee?	
Q6 Describe one area the manager could become more effective at when dealing with the employee?	
Q7 Overall what prevents the employee doing their job better?	
Q8 What should the manager keep doing?	

Key points

★ People are twice as likely to prefer receiving negative feedback compared to receiving positive feedback but, people are three times more likely to avoid giving negative feedback.

★ Managers and employees should have a regular one-on-one meeting schedule which includes qualitative and quantitative feedback in both directions.

Key Resources

★ "Your employees want the negative feedback you hate to give" - Harvard Business Review - Jack Zegner and Joseph Folkman

★ *The Ideal Team Player: How to Recognize and Cultivate The Three Essential Virtues* - Patrick Lencioni

★ *Multipliers: How the Best Leaders Make Everyone Smarter* - Liz Wiseman

3.3 Ideal Employee needs are identified and the Employee Promise is helping to attract the best employees at the pay you offer

Principle

On March 1 1914, Henry Ford announced that he was doubling the daily wage of his employees to $5 per day, much to the applause of the world's media. You've probably heard this story before, in the context of a generous profit sharing arrangement to enable workers to finally afford to buy the vehicles they were making, but what you might not know is that in the previous year Ford had a daily absenteeism rate of 10% and an annual staff turnover of 370%! With an average workforce of 13,600 employees, Ford had to employ 50,500 people annually simply to maintain the workforce. Clearly there were some serious employee-retention challenges the increase in wages was designed to overcome. The Ford assembly line was fantastic for productivity, but for an employee screwing the same nut onto the same chassis all day, every day, the monotony of the work was unbearable.

As dawn approached the day after the pay rise was announced, the thousands of people who were lined up outside to apply for the jobs began to enter the factory gates for job interviews to have their papers stamped by the interviewers and find out whether they were lucky enough to get a job. That's how the recruiting process worked then, the recruiting department would put the word out that they had jobs available, the word would get around town and people would queue up outside the gates. There was a large quantity of available workers for relatively few unskilled manual jobs where the employer held all the power and the workers held almost none.

Today, of course, the balance of power has shifted due to economic growth outstripping the availability of talented people and the transition to a knowledge-based economy. More companies are competing for the best talent in the belief that there is almost no substitute for a higher percentage of top performers. Ask any employer about the applicants they received for their last vacancy, and it's likely they found it difficult to fill the role because they received a large number of unsuitable applicants versus suitable applicants.

The most talented people are applying for the jobs with the best companies that give them what they need today, and, offer the best opportunity for career advancement in the future. They are applying for jobs that are in their own best interests.

In a study by Danny Samson from the University of Melbourne, 95% of employees said they would consistently put their own interests in front of those of their employer. Furthermore, only 8% would purely make decisions in the best interests of their employer. Most of the employees surveyed would choose an action that resulted in their employer forgoing $10 million if they personally gained at least $15,000.

While the high percentages are perhaps shocking, as a leader the fact that employees put their own interests first should come as no surprise to you. In fact, any sentient and emotionally aware leader should be surprised when employees don't act in their own interests.

In the same way that Nicolaus Copernicus demonstrated in 1543 that the Earth was not at the centre of the universe, your employees do not exist to revolve around you, and you are simply one part of a complex geocentric business model, along with your employees, revolving around the customer.

It's an important first step to accept that employees will, and in fact should, act in their own interests. That may require you to embrace your capability for humility and perhaps check your ego at the door, yet is fundamental for you to eventually become a magnet for the best talent.

Let's assume that you have now accepted that almost all employees both will and should act in their own interests. Using a first principles approach, if that is indeed true, then how does that change your approach to attracting and leading employees? If success in your job means leading a group of people who are most likely operating in their own interests, how can you get them to do their best work, with higher productivity and a higher retention rate?

You must understand what your ideal employees need from their place of work and consistently deliver it to them. This is done through an Employee Promise, a unique and measurable promise that meets the ideal employees needs, aligns with the Core Purpose as well as helping to deliver the Brand Promise.

In a 2001 Fortune magazine interview with Herb Kelleher, the CEO of Southwest Airlines famously said, 'You have to treat your employees like customers'. In the table below note how Southwest has interdependence between its Brand Promise and its Employee Promise.

SOUTHWEST AIRLINES BRAND PROMISE	SOUTHWEST AIRLINES EMPLOYEE PROMISE
★ Low fares	★ Lots of love
★ Lots of fun	★ Lots of fun
★ Lots of flights	★ Pro-active, co-dependent team

If we are to treat employees like customers, it begs the questions:

★ How do we treat our customers?
★ How do we attract customers?
★ How do we keep customers?

And can we emulate and align with our external client strategy, internally, to attract the best employees?

In order to attract and retain top performers to your organisation, you need more than tactics or gimmicks, you need a strategy. Using Michael Porter's definition of strategy in this context you need to create a unique and valuable position in the employer market, involving a different set of activities from your competitors for the same employees.

This simple and powerful Employee Promise concept was first introduced to me by the brilliant coach and my good friend Kevin Lawrence, author of the book, *Your Oxygen Mask First: 17 Habits to Help High Achievers Survive & Thrive in Leadership & Life*. Kevin and I have both used this concept successfully with our clients, helping to drive greater retention and productivity rates.

Creating and sustaining a unique and valuable position which meets the needs of both customers and employees is the balancing act of a thriving business. This is how strategy weaves with culture and your ideologies in the tapestry that is your company. You need to balance a strategy that creates a unique and valuable position externally to attract the right customers that align with your purpose, and you need a second strategy that creates a unique and valuable position internally to attract the employees who also align with your purpose and deliver that Core Purpose to your customers. But these two strategies are inter-dependent. Each relies on the other for its own success and is enabled by the company's Core Purpose.

Imagine the Core Purpose of your organisation is the fulcrum at the centre of a long narrow board, like a see-saw or a teeter-totter. At one end you have employees inside the organisation, and at the other end you have customers outside the organisation. The Core Purpose, the fulcrum at the centre, provides the ability to deliver the needs of employees at one end and to deliver the needs of customers at the other.

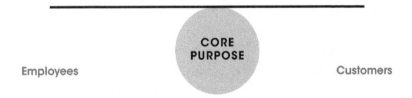

Now imagine a car dealership whose Core Purpose is to provide the best service in the city for prestige vehicles. Imagine that the marketing and the Brand Promises attracted the best customers in the city, customers who wanted the best service in the city for prestige vehicles – because they met the needs of those customers. But then the company didn't employ people who cared about the best service or about prestige vehicles. Employees were not aligned with the Core Purpose or Brand Promises, resulting in poor service. The fulcrum will not be in balance as shown in the diagram below. The employees won't align with the Core Purpose and Brand Promise, and the customers will eventually leave.

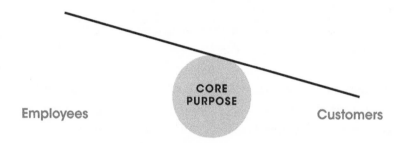

Now imagine a car dealership whose Core Purpose was to provide the lowest prices in the city for everyday vehicles. Imagine the marketing and the Brand Promises attracted the most price conscious customers in the city for their everyday vehicles. But the company only employed people who cared about the best service and prestige vehicles. Employees were not aligned with the Core Purpose or Brand Promises, which resulted in unhappy employees. The employees don't align with the Core Purpose and Brand Promise, and the employees will eventually leave.

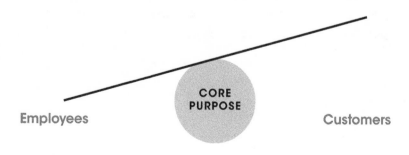

Let's consider Southwest Airlines again. The balance between getting the right employees who will live the Southwest Core Purpose and deliver the Brand Promises to Southwest customers is something that Southwest can uniquely deliver given the leadership, beliefs and culture it has developed over many years. The Southwest Core Purpose is to 'Connect people to what's important in their lives through friendly, reliable, and low-cost air travel.' How this is delivered to customers is through the three Brand Promises: Low fares, Lots of flights and Lots of fun.

In order to live this Core Purpose and deliver on these Brand Promises, Southwest attracts and retains the right people with three key Employee Promises: Lots of love, Lots of fun and a Proactive, codependent team. As shown below this provides a balance between the promises made to a customer, and the promises made to ideal employees who want to deliver these Brand Promises to customers.

Some potential employees might be qualified in every way to work for Southwest and might be drawn like a magnet because these Employee Promises, lots of love, lots of fun and pro-active, codependent team are exactly what they need. Others may be repelled, and that's okay. It's actually what you want from a good Employee Promise. Drawn from and connecting to both your Core Purpose and your Brand Promises, your Employee Promise should filter out the best candidates, attracting ideal employees seemingly like a magnet, while others are almost repelled, thinking they don't want to join your cult.

The key is that it takes a combination of both Brand Promises for customers and Employee Promises for employees to achieve balance and succeed as outlined in the diagram below.

SOUTHWEST AIRLINES

Lots of love   Lots of fun   Pro-active, codependent team   Lots of fun   Lots of flights   Low fares

CORE PURPOSE
Connect people to what's important in their lives through friendly, reliable, low-cost air travel

Employees

Customers

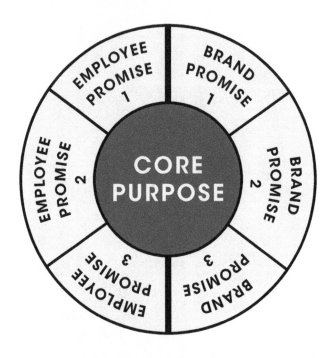

In Simon Sinek's book, *Start With Why: How Great Leaders Inspire Everyone to Take Action,* he introduced the concept of the Golden Circle, outlining the importance of why, or Core Purpose, and the importance of it being at the centre of an organisation's perspective. Furthermore, Sinek stated that most organisations know what they do, few know how they do it, and very few organisations know why they do what they do.

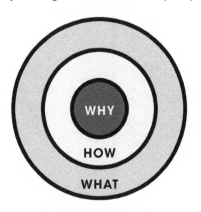

When we translate the Golden Circle and realise that how, the second circle, consists of the promises we make to both customers and employees enabling the delivery through our sandbox – what we do, we then consider the diagram below.

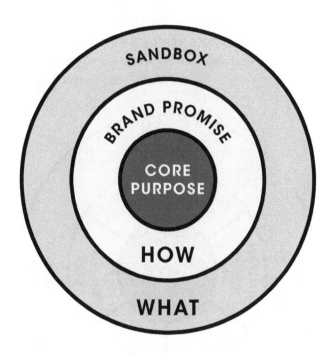

Finally we can complete the diagram by incorporating the four key elements of the sandbox, the 'what' you do. This includes:

★ **SALES TERRITORY** – where you will sell
★ **PRODUCT LINES** – what you will sell
★ **IDEAL CUSTOMER** – who you will sell to
★ **IDEAL EMPLOYEE** – who will sell and deliver

To summarise, there are three circles a small one inside a medium one which in turn is inside a large one. At the centre, in the smallest circle is your Core Purpose, the reason your company exists. Outside that, in the middle is how you do what you do, and this circle is split into six segments consisting of three Brand Promises and three Employee Promises. Then the largest circle, your sandbox or how you will deliver consists of your sales territory, where you will sell, your product lines, what you will sell, your ideal customer, who you will sell to, and finally your ideal employee, who will sell and deliver your product.

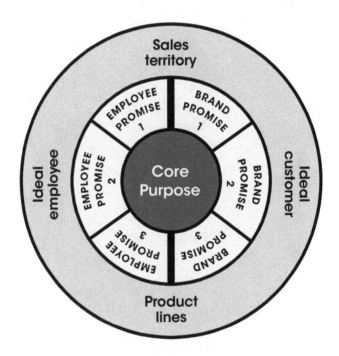

Story

Carly and Eric Cohen, clients from Maple group, operate two of Melbourne's top wedding venues and have built a great culture. Such a good culture that the leadership team were incredibly proud to be listed as one of Australia's Best Places to Work for two consecutive years, and again for a third year in 2018.

Despite this, Carly and Eric found it difficult to find top performers for frontline jobs. The job advertising was fine, they had an acceptable number of applicants and the filtering process to convert the right candidates into employees was good. Yet not enough top performers were applying to meet the demands of the business. The process and tactics to employ people was working, but there wasn't alignment between the strategy to attract customers and the strategy to attract employees.

Put simply, Maple's Brand Promise was to 'wow' the brides and guests at the weddings and events their venues hosted. Everyone in the business just loved to impress their guests and make their events special. The walls of the business were literally covered in stories about employees who wowed their customers, living the Maple Core Values and Core Purpose.

As a strategy, we had to find employees who were motivated by this purpose, to find employees who had a deep-seated need to wow the guests at events. Maple's company culture was unique and valuable already and therefore our focus was to clearly understand who the ideal employee would be, that was motivated by this purpose, and what their needs were.

We identified that the ideal employee had three needs that could become an Employee Promise. First, they had a deep-seated need to create a wow experience with a fun team. Second, they desired recognition and feedback and third they needed to be part of a team that provides lots of love.

From there Carly and Eric were able to develop Maple's employer branding using the Employee Promise, and build out the tactics to attract more top performers.

MAPLE GROUP EMPLOYEE PROMISE

Tool

The circle diagram below is also represented in the worksheet below. On the left is the ideal employee. On the right is the ideal customer. Your job is to deliver on ideal customer needs and ideal employee needs while enhancing the Core Purpose of the organisation.

You connect the ideal employee needs with the Core Purpose of the organisation through a unique and measurable Employee Promise. This Employee Promise is HOW you will engage your WHAT to your

WHY. By living the Core Purpose, and delivering on the Employee Promise you should be meeting the ideal employee needs.

You connect the ideal customer needs with the Core Purpose of the organisation through a unique and measurable Brand Promise. This Brand Promise is HOW you will sell your WHAT to your WHO. By living the Core Purpose, and delivering on the Brand Promise, you should be meeting the Ideal Customer needs.

The Brand Promise and the ideal customer needs are developed later in the Strategy section of this book. In order to complete the customer side of this tool you may need to complete the tool in section 4.3.

In order to complete the employee side of this tool complete the steps below.

★ What is your sandbox. What will you sell? Who will you sell to? Where will you sell?

★ What is your Core Purpose? Why does your company exist?

★ What are the characteristics of the ideal employee, and what does this person need, not want, from an organisation like yours?

★ What three Employee Promises can you make that are unique, measurable and meet the ideal employees needs?

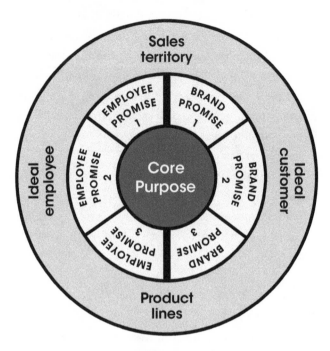

Adapted from Simon Sinek *Start with Why*

After you have completed the Employee Promise section on the left and you have completed Brand Promise and ideal customer needs from Chapter 4, complete this chart and review all to ensure that you have an alignment and interdependence through each of these sections, that indeed your Employee Promise is meeting the needs of the ideal employee, living the Core Purpose and helping to deliver on the ideal customer needs.

Employee Promise Tool

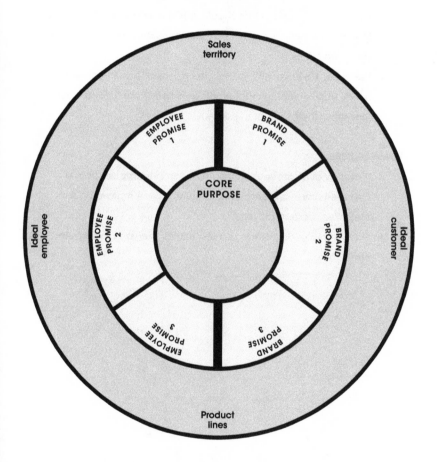

Key points

- ★ More companies are competing for the best talent in the belief that there is almost no substitute for a higher percentage of top performers.
- ★ Employees will, and in fact should, act in their own best interests.
- ★ Meeting the need for your ideal customers is ultimately done by your employees.
- ★ Therefore, it is important to align the needs of employees with the needs of customers, in that employees needs are fulfilled when they meet the needs of customers.

Key Resources

- ★ University of Melbourne - https://www.smartcompany.com.au/people-human-resources/much-money-take-employee-put-interests-ahead-employers/
- ★ *Start With Why: How Great Leaders Inspire Everyone to Take Action* - Simon Sinek

3.4 Employee Promise KPIs are measured weekly and performance is displayed all around the business

Principle

For the 2018 annual CEO survey, PWC interviewed 1,344 CEOs from around the world and the statistics around their talent strategies were disturbing. The data demonstrated that:

- ★ 63% of CEOs are concerned about finding talent with key skills
- ★ 93% say they recognise the need to change their strategies for talent
- ★ 61% haven't taken the first step to change their strategies for talent

The year prior, the survey showed that 77% of CEOs had plans to change their talent strategies, and a similar story had been told in the previous eight years. According to the report, 'every year, their concerns about availability of talent have increased. CEOs are well aware that something needs to be done, but are less sure of exactly what that is.'

So why might finding talented employees be a problem?

Let's consider it from the employee's perspective.

According to the 2018 Edelman Trust Barometer 80% of employees trust their industry sector more that they trust their employer, and furthermore, of the 20% who trust their employer more than their sector, it was only by an average 3 percentage point margin.

Employees want to trust their employers, but often they aren't provided any meaningful reason to do so. Trust isn't something you obtain automatically once an employee signs your employment contract; trust must be earned.

Presenting an Employee Promise and delivering it in an authentic manner will not only help to meet the needs of your employees, but measuring it regularly and making the data public will increase trust with employees, thereby improving retention and productivity rates.

If you understand the needs of your ideal employees, and you make three unique and measurable Employee Promises that align with these needs, your job then is to execute consistently on these Employee Promises. There is no quicker way to erode trust and upset your employees than to promise something that meets their needs and then fail to deliver on it.

How then can a leader execute the Employee Promises?

In his book *Mastering the Rockefeller Habits*, Verne Harnish outlined the three disciplines that lead to good execution:

- ★ **PRIORITIES** - having everyone in the organisation knowing the top three to five priorities for the company, department and each individual
- ★ **METRICS / DATA** - having the right data to make the right decisions at the right time
- ★ **MEETING RHYTHM** - having a regular rhythm of daily / weekly / monthly / quarterly meetings to improve communication and increase the pulse of the team's decision making

If we consider how to execute the Employee Promise in this context we have:

- ★ **PRIORITIES** - have everyone in the business know that the Employee Promise is a priority because it is displayed all around the business on posters and dashboards
- ★ **METRICS** - dashboards throughout the business are displaying Employee Promise KPI's
- ★ **MEETING RHYTHM** - at each weekly meeting for the leadership team the latest results from the Employee Promise KPIs are updated and discussed

This is a system that will ultimately align the activities of your business with the needs of your ideal employees. Remember that an Employee Promise isn't a tagline, it's how you will engage your 'why' to your 'who', and it results in higher retention and higher productivity. Employees want to work for you because you meet their needs better than anyone else, and you are better at it than any other organisation.

But this system must be maintained. It's like brushing your teeth. It's not a once in a while thing: it's an all-the-time thing. The promises you make to employees must be delivered or maintained 24 hours a day, 7 days a week. Your goal is to try and avoid the credibility chasm, that is the difference between what you say (your Employee Promise) and what you do in the eyes of your employees.

If your Employee Promise is displayed all around the business, and the results are discussed each week, your recruitment team can use it as a legitimate and authentic tool with candidates.

Story

The first time I met James was in a crowded coffee shop just outside the city. I had worked with a friend of his for a few years, and he suggested we meet, knowing that I might be able to help with some of the challenges that James was having in his business. About ten minutes after our agreed meeting time, James arrived, making a brief excuse about having a busy day and the state of the traffic. As a person who helps teams improve their discipline and knowing that the CEO is the custodian of organisational discipline, I found his lateness very interesting and wondered whether this was indeed an abnormal meeting, or if James generally ran late. James ordered, and we sat down to enjoy a coffee in order to learn about one another.

With just over 80 employees James' business had operated for about 14 years and provided components for the building industry. After we discussed his sales and organisational structure, the subject moved onto people and he said, 'I don't have a culture, we're just a group of guys and girls who work together'.

'That's like saying you don't have a personality', I replied. 'And while it might be hard to detect, even bureaucrats have a personality!'

Even though you might not consciously work on your company culture, even if you treat your employees terribly, your company will always have a company culture. Imagine one of your employees is at a barbeque on the weekend with friends, discussing your business as a place of work, when their friend asks, 'I've heard of that company, so what's it like to work there?'. The response to that question is an example of your employees describing your company culture.

If you don't consciously build and manage your company culture, you'll likely end up with a culture that isn't attracting and retaining the best talent and creating the great business you are hoping to build.

James laughed. 'I guess you're right', he said. 'But we've always thought that we've got good people and our culture was okay, and that we didn't really need to do anything more at this point. I guess we always thought that dedicating time to culture was only for larger companies?'.

I replied, 'The data shows that the top-performing employees in any industry will stay for longer and achieve higher productivity rates in organisations with demonstrably higher culture ratings'.

I let James ponder that for a few moments before I started enquiring about any initiatives that he had started with his company for employees. 'Tell me, is there anything you have done to try and build your culture? Are there any initiatives you have undertaken to build a better workplace?' I paused sensing James' uncertainty about how to respond to the question. 'Perhaps an annual dinner with staff, or even a bonus scheme?'.

'Oh, sure', James replied, 'we all go to lunch before we break for summer holidays when we're closed for three weeks, and,' he paused, almost as if he knew he was about to say something negative about his culture 'we were looking at a bonus scheme a couple of years ago, but we couldn't get it to work'.

My mind recalled how James was ten minutes late, and I wondered again how often he was late to meetings as I enquired, 'tell me more about that?'.

'Well I had read about providing a percentage of profits to staff as an incentive, and to help prevent staff leaving. I built a program to share 20% of our after-tax profits amongst staff, we put it out there and it just didn't work.' he said.

'You put it out there?' I enquired.

'Yes, we ran a meeting where I discussed the profit share arrangement but then in the first quarter we made a loss, so I couldn't share a loss, anyway from there we just didn't really talk about it again.' he said.

'And that was 2 years ago?' I confirmed.

'Yes', he replied, beginning to see where I was heading.

'Can you think of any other examples where you have started an initiative, like the profit share, where you have discussed an initiative that might benefit employees, and then that initiative wasn't fully and successfully executed?' I asked.

'There have been a few, I guess that's why I'm here, I'm looking for help.'

I wondered briefly if I should look deeper into these other instances, but I knew that James could see the pattern and that was all that mattered.

'James, when it comes to people, either customers or employees, we are looking to build trust. Trust is earned or lost with credibility, what I call the credibility chasm, which is the difference between your words and your actions. Every time you make a commitment and don't deliver on it you erode trust proportional to the size of the commitment. So if you arrive ten minutes late to a meeting you erode trust a little, but if you promise employees a pay rise and don't deliver on it, you erode trust a lot.'

I allowed the silence of the following moment to just hang there and work it's magic as James contemplated what I had said, how I had identified a serious cultural problem that may be a reason behind his

Quarterly Employee Promise dashboard

	EMPLOYEE PROMISE 1	EMPLOYEE PROMISE 2	EMPLOYEE PROMISE 3
WEEKLY TARGET GREEN/RED			
Week 1			
Week 2			
Week 3			
Week 4			
Week 5			
Week 5			
Week 6			
Week 7			
Week 8			
Week 9			
Week 10			
Week 11			
Week 12			
Week 13			

high turnover rate, how perhaps he hadn't contemplated it from this angle before, and how this person he had only just met had held him accountable in a way that no one else had in his life for a very long time. I could see his initial reaction was to defend his lateness, but his curiosity, and knowledge that there was in fact a chance that I could be right, prevented him from defending both his lateness and the trust deficiency within his employees we were to later validate.

Tool

If you're not willing to accept the pain a real Employee Promise incurs, and to measure it consistently over time, don't bother going to the trouble of formulating an Employee Promise. You'll be better off without one. But if you have the fortitude to see it through, there are a few important lessons you can learn from.

First, ask for flexibility from employees. A tree whose branches aren't flexible in the wind of a storm will simply break. As strong as trees appear, they must be flexible in order to survive. Explain to employees that you are trying the Employee Promise and want to make it work, but that it may require changes and improvements over time. Don't sign yourself up to a rigid commitment you may regret.

Second, appoint an owner of your Employee Promise project, ideally outside the leadership team. This person will ultimately be responsible for ensuring that the KPI's are updated weekly and data makes its way to weekly leadership team meetings for discussion. Allocate time in your weekly meeting agenda to discuss Employee Promise KPIs.

Finally, after measuring for a few quarters, set yourself a target, a green / red so that everyone knows how you are performing on each Employee Promise each week. But only after you have enough data from a few quarters to be able to make an educated decision.

Over time you can measure the Employee Promise KPIs and publish them all around the business using a table like the one below to track performance.

Key points

★ CEOs are concerned about finding talent with the right skills, yet often don't take action to improve their talent strategies.

★ Employees trust in their employers is often damaged by failed employer initiatives or commitments.

★ Transparently measuring Employee Promises improves trust and recruitment initiatives.

Key Resources

★ PWC CEO Survey - https://www.pwc.com/gx/en/ceo-agenda/ceosurvey/2018/au

★ Edelman Trust Barometer 2018 - https://www.edelman.com/trust-barometer

★ *Mastering the Rockefeller Habits: What You Must Do to Increase the Value of Your Growing Firm* - Verne Harnish

3.5 Where Core Values breaches occur employees are reprimanded or terminated

Principle

In his book *Built to Last: Successful habits of Visionary Companies* Jim Collins describes Core Values as the shared, deeply held beliefs of the leaders in the businesses he studied.

'Hewlett, Packard, Merck, Johnson, and Watson didn't sit down and ask "What business values would maximise our wealth?" or "What philosophy would look nice printed on glossy paper?" or "What beliefs would please the financial community?" ', he writes 'No! They articulated what was inside them - what was in their gut, what was bone deep. It was as natural to them as breathing. It's not what they believed as much as how deeply they believed it (and how consistently the organisation lived it). Again, the key word is authenticity. No artificial flavours. No added sweeteners. Just 100 percent genuine authenticity.'

Collins further defines Core Values as 'the organisations essential and enduring tenets, not to be compromised for financial gain or short term expediency'.

So in the event these genuinely held, deep-as-bone beliefs that are shared amongst the leadership team are breached in your organisation, are you creating a consequence for the culprit?

In 1400 Geoffrey Chaucer wrote in his collection of stories, *The Canterbury Tales*:

'About an old proverb, the words that say:
"A rotten apple's better thrown away
Before it spoils the barrel." That is true
When dealing with a bad apprentice too.'

We can take from this quote that well over 600 years ago management techniques dictated that an employee with a bad attitude would 'spoil' a group of employees and that the 'spoiled' employee should be removed before they spoil the entire group.

Let's take a look at a much later version of this saying: 'One bad apple can ruin a box of apples, but one good apple won't make a box of bad apples good again'. As is often the case if you have a group of employees with a bad attitude, putting an employee with a good attitude into the group won't convert the bad attitudes.

And yet in today's corporate world reprimands or dismissals for employees who breach Core Values are still quite rare. But it doesn't need to be this way. One of the main reasons that leaders don't reprimand or terminate employees due to Core Values breaches is that the Core Values are not strong enough in the organisation. It is simply unfair to hold a person accountable to a set of behavioural expectations that the person isn't aware of, or are not well known throughout the company. Be certain though, we are not talking about terminating employees for failing to live the Core Values, we are talking about terminating for *breaching* the Core Values. If one of your Core Values was 'Motivated' for example, that you valued team members who were motivated, the suggestion is not that one should terminate employees who aren't motivated, who turned up and did a good job. However, perhaps if you had a serial offender who consistently was a de-motivator for colleagues, who consistently breached the motivated Core Value, that person might not belong in the organisation.

As outlined in the first section of this culture chapter, it is the role of the CEO and leadership team to ensure everyone in the organisation understands the Core Values and Core Purpose. Once your team understands these and they are not only able to recite them, but able to connect each value with lived stories giving them a deep understanding of the meaning, you can begin to outline what behaviours align with being right and wrong when referring to the Core Values.

To ensure everyone at Netflix was clear on behavioural expectations, CEO Reed Hasting created a Core Values and culture slide deck explicitly outlining the values and culture expectations for Netflix people. The quote below from the Netflix deck demonstrates how Hastings publicly outlines why they fire people.

> 'Adequate performance gets a generous severance package.
> We're a team, not a family.
> We're like a pro sports team, not a kid's recreational team.
> Netflix leaders hire, develop and cut smartly, so we have stars in every position.
> The Keeper Test managers use:
> Which of my people,
> If they told me they were leaving for a similar job at a peer company, would I fight hard to keep at Netflix?
> The other people should get a generous severance now,
> So that we can open a slot to try to find a star for that role.'

The expectation at Netflix is that if you wouldn't fight hard to keep one of your people, they should exit now. But the deck is clear that this is not only for productivity reasons, the deck goes on to define what a high performer who doesn't embody the Core Values is called, 'a brilliant jerk', and that Netflix won't tolerate brilliant jerks as the cost to teamwork is too high.

How has providing this clarity on behavioural and cultural expectations helped the Netflix culture? According to Comparably, a culture comparison website, Netflix ranks first on the overall culture score rank, with a score of 82/100, as well as first on the employee Net Promoter Score (eNPS) rank against its competitors Facebook, Google, Amazon, Apple and Hulu.

Furthermore CEO Reed Hastings also ranks first against competitor CEOs in the 'CEO Ratings comparison' with Sundar Pichai in second (Google), Tim Cook in third (Apple), Mark Zuckerberg in fourth (Facebook), Jeff Bezos in fifth (Amazon) and Randy Freer in sixth (Hulu).

The Netflix Core Values and culture slide deck makes it abundantly clear about the positive and negative expectations of employees in terms of both performance and values alignment.

Story

Nicola was so frustrated and angry she could barely maintain our conversation.

'He just doesn't get it', she said, 'No one wants to work with him, and he blames everyone else when things go wrong!' she continued.

Craig, the manager who Nicola was talking about, had been cited once again as a reason for an employee leaving during an exit interview. Craig wasn't the exiting employees' manager, but they often interacted in their roles. In the few years I had worked with Nicola we had discussed Craig and his negative impact on the business many times.

'So many people in the business just don't deal with him', she said, 'They just don't want to have any involvement, so they refuse to communicate with him at all. That's got to be hurting the business.'

I allowed her to vent her frustrations completely. It took a few more minutes until eventually she was done.

'How much damage is Craig causing the business culture, and where is the line in the sand? The point at which enough is enough?' I asked, knowing the enormous damage that Craig had already caused. Unfortunately, this triggered Nicola to vent her frustrations even further.

'You know, it's probably been twenty people. Twenty good people we have lost because Craig has absolutely no idea how to even interact with other people, let alone be a decent manager!' She continued, 'Of course then there are the people who haven't left but aren't happy. That's before we even start to think about the productivity cost on the whole company'.

I was very familiar with all of this. Nicola and I had discussed Craig on many occasions. In fact I have had conversations just like this with many CEOs about culturally poor performing employees over the years. Craig was the typical 'brilliant jerk' described by Reed Hastings from Netflix. Craig would consistently achieve his KPIs and was a key part of the businesses' recent growth, and we both knew that. I continued and pressed my original question, 'So where is the line in the sand? When does enough become enough?'

Nicola paused, longer than her normal pause. I suspect it was because she was calming down to try and offer a meaningful answer.

'The problem is that he is just so hard to replace, the technical work that he does with clients is great, and the clients love him.' I'd heard that before and she knew it. Nicola and I had long before established that our relationship was built on brutal honesty and she was conscious that we would need to go deeper. 'Not all of the clients', she added, 'a few have asked to not deal with him, but still, our biggest clients love him and I don't know if we can afford to break the relationships he has with them.'

'So the real problem here is not that Craig is an incompetent leader who doesn't align with our Core Values, the real problem is that you feel trapped. Your source of frustration is not that you have a problem employee, but that you feel powerless to take action and improve the situation.'

'If he left it would be so hard to replace him', Nicola said agreeing. The exasperation in her voice implied that she was hoping for some way to break the stalemate.

I paused, choosing my words carefully, a little like the actor Bill Murray in the movie 'Groundhog day' trying to find a way to escape living the same situation over and over.

'One day, Craig won't work here', I said, waiting for her to respond.

'Yes', she replied with hesitation.

'Let's assume that is 4 years away', I said, 'He has been here for 5 years and let's assume he is here for another 4 years'.

'Okay', she replied.

'Is he going to resign, or will he be fired?' I asked thereby forcing her to realise her tolerance of the situation, the fact the she is in control of this situation and that eventually she will need to hire a person to replace Craig.

'I guess', she said, 'either he is going to get a job somewhere else and resign, or he is going to do something so bad that I will be forced to sack him.'

'How bad?' I enquired.

'Bad enough that our lawyers are involved. You know, bullying, theft or sexual misconduct,' she said, absorbing what she was saying.

'In four years time, Craig is gone. What is the cost you are going to pay in the next 48 months in damage to your company?'

'A lot', she replied.

'So in 48 months after he has gone you still need to replace him, you can either replace him now and begin to rebuild your culture, productivity and retention rates, or you can spend the money to enable Craig to further damage the company and start rebuilding in 4 years', I said.

Nicola reclined in her high back directors chair, contemplating this decision she had debated in her mind so many times before. She thought for what must have been three minutes before she spoke next.

'Okay, let's do it. I will give him a written warning tonight.'

I smiled because for Nicola, like so many CEOs, she felt trapped and had made the decision to take action to improve her culture by exiting the brilliant jerk.

At our next meeting a month later, I enquired about Craig and how things were progressing. Craig had resigned during the meeting where he received a written warning, and Nicola was in the final stages of recruiting a replacement who was both technically capable and she felt aligned with the Core Values. Also, Nicola noted that there was a noticeable lift in the mood of other employees.

Tool

Tony Hsieh, CEO of Zappos, is quoted as saying, 'If you don't fire people for not following the Core Values, they become a meaningless plaque on the wall.'

But how?

How can you evolve from having Core Values truly alive in your organisation, a worthy goal for any leader in itself, to being confident that you would fire a person for breaching the values? You need to define what it means to not live the values, and what breaching the values represents. Employees need to understand both the positive and negative aspects of your Core Values.

In the worksheet below write your Core Values in the first row entitled 'List your values'.

Then starting with your first value, consider ways in which people live this value, and come up with 3 ideas to explain how people live this value in the next row.

For example if your value is 'Got your back - support each other' the three ways people live this value might be:

1. We ask colleagues if they need help if they seem to be in trouble.
2. We take work from team members to help the whole team achieve goals
3. We challenge colleagues in a respectful way to be the best they can

Next consider 3 examples how people don't live the Core Values.

Using the same example 'Got your back - support each other' here are another 3 examples:

1. We compete against other departments for resources or favour with management
2. 'Sink or Swim' behaviour where someone has to lose for you to win
3. We allow people to accept mediocre results or performance

Finally consider 3 examples of why someone would expect disciplinary action relating to this value. Using the same example 'Got your back - support each other' here are another 3 examples:

1. You promote one part of the business winning at the expense of others
2. You fail to help your teammates in a situation where they may need help
3. You fail to ask team mates for help and subsequently fail on a project

Core Values accountability worksheet

LIST YOUR VALUES >	CORE VALUE 1	CORE VALUE 2	CORE VALUE 3	CORE VALUE 4	CORE VALUE 5	CORE VALUE 6	CORE VALUE 7
Our people live this value when **a.**							
b.							
c.							
Our people don't live this value when **a.**							
b.							
c.							
You can expect disciplinary action relating to this value when **a.**							
b.							
c.							

Key points

★ Core Values represent the few, deepest held behavioural beliefs of an organisation's leaders.

★ Reprimands or dismissals for employees who breach Core Values are often quite rare.

★ People who regularly breach the Core Values are likely to continue to breach, thereby further damaging the culture and should be exited.

Key Resources

★ *Built to Last: Successful Habits of Visionary Companies* - Jim Collins and Jerry I. Porras

★ *The Canterbury Tales* - Geoffrey Chaucer

★ Comparably Netflix culture comparison - https://www.comparably.com/companies/netflix/competitors

★ STRATEGY

4.0 The company's strategy delivers a unique and valuable position in the marketplace which is different to competitors

Over the years, I must have asked hundreds of CEOs and leadership teams the question 'Can you explain your strategy in a sentence?' I would estimate that less than 1% actually have a strategy, even if they can't explain it in a sentence. That is, a strategy to create a unique and valuable position in the marketplace which is different to competitors.

The inconvenient reality is that most leadership teams are constantly distracted by operations. So much of what occurs in the day-to-day operations of a business comes from what Stephen Covey would call quadrant 1 from his book *The 7 Habits of Highly Effective People*. These are things that are important and urgent.

These operational distractions include:

★ Attracting sufficient customer enquiries
★ Selling enough to meet budget
★ Manufacturing or ordering the right amount at the right time
★ Delivering on time
★ Invoicing and collecting payment on time

Each and every day, leaders and managers arrive at their office to work through a never-ending list of day-to-day operational activities. They believe that working through these operational activities will see them doing a good job.

But great businesses are not built that way. That's the way to build a mediocre business, or a good business at best.

Instead leaders should be spending their time in Covey's quadrant 2, working on things that are important and not urgent. The thing that is most important and yet not urgent is the company strategy.

The problem is that over the past 40 years, strategy has become one of the most important drivers of market value as displayed in the chart below. In 1975 83% of the S&P 500 market value consisted of tangible assets, items such as land, vehicles and machinery - things that can be touched.

By 2015 only 13% of the S&P 500 market value consisted of tangible assets, with 87% being intangible assets such as patents, trademarks, goodwill and copyright.

TANGIBLE VS. INTANGIBLE COMPONENETS OF THE S&P 500 MARKET VALUE (%)

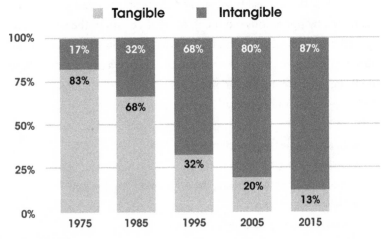

Source: BAML

Developing a strategy providing you a unique and valuable position in the market doesn't come about by dedicating your thinking time to buying more machinery, vehicles and buildings. Sure they create value, but they are a function of leveraging your balance sheet, your actual ability to purchase, whereas the value created from intangible assets comes about by working to develop something unique. This is the output of strategic thinking.

That doesn't mean you should drop everything and start work on a patent. But it does mean that you should begin to appreciate the importance of strategy in building your company value and the distinct possibility that you are not currently working to evolve a strategy in your business.

You may look at the data above and consider that in fact intangible growth has come about by technology and not strategy. However, it should be considered that the word strategy only really started appearing in prominent management literature in the 1960s. In fact much of what we know today about strategy has come about since the 1980s, through the work of people such as Michael Porter and Jim Collins.

I contend that the maturation and adoption of strategy principles has had a lot to do with intangible assets representing such a large portion of the S&P 500 value.

Of course new technology always creates opportunities that were not previously present. When Henry Ford created operational efficiencies through the assembly line, he had a major advantage over competitors. When we look at the chart below, the top 5 publicly traded companies by market cap in 2001, 2006 and 2011 had only one tech company, yet in 2016 all five were tech companies. It's easy to say that is because they were tech companies, but I propose it was because they had a strong strategy.

Microsoft was on the list in 2001 and 2006 because it had a unique and valuable position in its market. In 2000, 95% of personal computers and smartphones used a Microsoft operating system. By 2010 that

TOP 5 PUBLICLY TRADED COMPANIES

(by market cap)

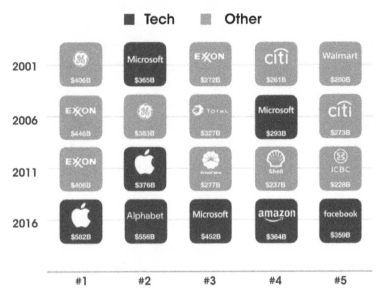

was 70%. By 2011 it was down to 50%. That 20% drop was primarily attributed to the success of the iPhone which in 2011 saw Apple rise to second spot and then the first spot in 2016. This is because Apple held a unique and valuable position in the market, so valuable in fact that they attracted 83% of the smartphone industry profits in 2017.

Apple doesn't have better technology than its competitors, certainly not to the extent that it should attract such a large percentage of industry profits, it simply has a better strategy that sets it apart, that lets it own a white space no one else can compete in.

For Alphabet, the owner of Google, it could be argued that the search algorithm is better than Bing or any other competitor, but its strategy to be the first place to search the internet, by being on computer manufacturer's browsers, and by owning that space, and by making advertisers pay to appear on the Google homepage, that is what has driven its success.

Also, Amazon may have a better recommendation engine than its competitors, but its strategy to relentlessly focus on low prices, fast delivery and lots of products would have been a winning strategy well before the internet existed.

Finally, Facebook may have good technology to view photos and videos, but the strategy to create a community where all your friends and relatives share their photos and life events is a strategy that is almost impossible to compete with – users don't want to leave because everyone else is there.

The point is you can look at the success of tech companies and think they are valuable because of technology, or you can think they are valuable because of their strategy. My reasoning is that they have won because they created a unique and valuable position in the market. They executed a winning strategy.

It just happens to leverage tech.

Every business is simply people, making, buying and selling things to other people. You can develop a winning strategy in your business, but remember that strategy isn't something that you get, it isn't something that you lock in the safe or drawer after attending a two-hour speaking event. Strategy is an evolution over time around certain principles to put you in the white space where no one else competes.

All of the the companies listed above in the market cap graph are successful not because they are tech companies but because they have evolved their strategy over time to the point where they now own a unique and valuable position in the market that is different than their competitors.

In today's rapidly changing world the challenge is for executives and CEOs to always be seeking the next unique and valuable position in markets they already operate in, thereby potentially jeopardizing their existing business. As the American writer Upton Sinclair said. 'It is difficult to get a man to understand something, when his salary depends upon his not understanding it!'

And we see that story played out again and again through companies like Blockbuster and Kodak, once industry titans who at one point had a winning strategy, but treated strategy as something that is built, rather than something that must be continually built and evolved through a process.

As a CEO, your job is to own a process which discovers and executes on activities that see your firm become unique in the marketplace.

Key points

- ★ Many leadership teams spend all their time on operational matters, and little to no time working on their strategy.
- ★ Real value in a firm comes from having a unique and valuable position in the market, a position that is different from competitors, which is ultimately the output of strategy.
- ★ Strategy is a constantly iterative process, which is always ongoing, and is informed by execution.

Key Resources

- ★ *The 7 Habits of Highly Effective People: Powerful Lessons in Personal Change* - Stephen Covey

4.1 Quarterly and annually the leadership team meets offsite to reflect, evolve the company strategy and set priorities

Principle

Building a strategy is a little like exercising.

You don't need to exercise, in fact many people don't.

You shouldn't spend a whole day at the gym and think that you don't need to exercise any more. It just won't work.

If you maintain a habit of regular exercise, gradually you will see the benefits.

Jack Welch, arguably the most successful CEO of all time, having grown General Electric by over 4000% in twenty years describes strategy in his book *Jack: Straight from the Gut* as 'The evolution of a central idea through continually changing circumstances'.

Or the evolution and adaptability of a strategy is perhaps put less eloquently by the boxer Mike Tyson when he said, 'Everyone has a plan until they get punched in the mouth!'.

According to the Editorial Director of Harvard Business School Publishing and author of the book *Lords of Strategy: The Secret Intellectual History of the New Corporate World,* Walter Kiechel, 90% of strategies fail due to poor execution, but is it really the fault of the execution, or the inflexibility of the strategy? A quote from Harvard Business School, by Professor Bill Sullivan, stated 'At Harvard Business School I saw 5,000 business plans and only three were executed. They we were all great teams and all pivoted - this is why you need 90-day plans not three-year plans'.

It's important to understand the difference between strategic thinking and execution planning, and why many people recommend the phrase 'strategic planning' not be used any more.

Strategic thinking is the evolution of the central ideas within your strategy over time. In the words of the famous Harvard Business School

Professor Michael Porter, 'to develop and maintain a unique and valuable position, involving a different set of activities from competitors'.

That's where the name of my company 'Evolution Partners' came from. A great company is built not from a 'Growth Hack' or attending a one day workshop. A great company is built through conscious discipline and the evolution of a strategy over time.

Execution planning is the process of determining the priorities and goals that will progress toward your strategy in the next 90 days. The top three to five priorities, the priorities for the entire company and for each department which are not urgent, but are important according to Stephen Covey as mentioned in the introduction to this section are decided by the leadership team at a quarterly offsite planning workshop. Then these priorities, which outline *what* the company must achieve is shared with all managers, supervisors and workers throughout the company. In the first week following the quarterly workshop managers and their teams decide *how* they will execute on these priorities by building a 13-week plan for each priority complete with weekly milestones.

So after the quarterly planning offsite workshop the priorities descend the org chart as shown in the diagram below.

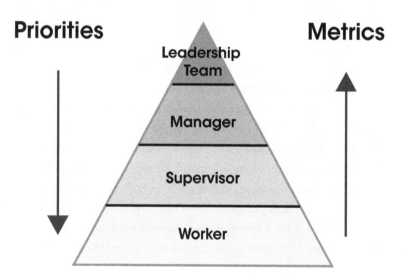

Then as the quarter progresses the measurement of these priorities, which is effectively working *on* the business along with the KPIs from people's roles which measure people working *in* the business is collated and these metrics will ascend the org chart throughout the quarter.

After a quarterly execution planning meeting, priorities are shared downward and then during the quarter metrics – the reporting of people's progress working both on and in the business – are shared upward.

So in the background there is a constant evolution of the strategy, like a labourer who is digging an ever-larger moat around the castle that is your business, the moat of course being the unique and valuable position you are obtaining in the market, undertaking a different set of activities from competitors.

In the foreground is the 90-day plan. An ongoing series of 90-day sprints with three to five priorities for the business as a whole and three to five priorities for each part of the business. These priorities are set each 90 days because the business is ever changing, but broadly should align with the longer term strategy that is evolving in the background, along with the current internal and external environment.

That's what Jack Welch learned at General Electric, that traditional business plans just don't work. People labour over a five-year plan, and once it's complete they stick it in a drawer and it just gathers dust. When Jack built the famous GE training facility at Crotonville, New York, he mandated that plans should be simple enough to fit onto one page and should operate in 90-day sprints.

People ask, 'Does the planning session need to be offsite, as we have a great boardroom?' Yes, in fact for people I work with this is one of the rules I just won't budge on, because it doesn't matter where it is, but the difference in taking a leadership team outside the office not only sends a clear message that we are here to think strategically and undertake execution planning, but it also avoids the distractions of the office. If you can't afford the best room at the Four Seasons hotel then don't book it, book a YMCA or a library, or borrow a friend's boardroom. Just don't do yourself a disservice and treat it like every other meeting.

Should you facilitate yourself or engage an external coach?

There are three main reasons you should engage a professional coach to facilitate your quarterly and annual offsite workshops.

First, the CEO is one of the smartest and most experienced people in the room. If you are facilitating you are not focussed on the creative thinking, you are worried about presenting, managing relationships and managing time.

Second, if you are standing at the front of the room, it is very difficult to engender genuine debate. It is simply not possible to facilitate a debate and participate in a debate at the same time.

Third, the CEO is the boss. If your boss is standing at the front of the room, running the meeting and telling you what he thinks the company should do, it is very easy for delegates to simply capitulate and not enter into a healthy debate.

The people who build the plan don't fight the plan, and so to get support for your 90-day plan it's critical to achieve healthy debate from all leadership team members.

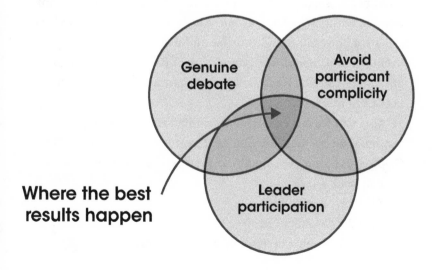

If you need help from a premium coach to facilitate your off-site workshops I'd be happy to introduce you to some of our certified coaching partners across the globe.

Story

My hometown Perth is a mining city. The general financial health of the entire state economy and even the Government finances are directly connected to cyclical commodity prices and mining investment. And the last seven years has been a rollercoaster. To put this in context in 2011 Western Australia had its highest-ever mining investment at around $50 billion. Two years later that had almost doubled to $95 billion. In 2017 that had plummeted back to $45 billion.

This massive growth and subsequent decline has hollowed out the economy with businesses collapsing, home prices dropping and a lot of 'unhealthy' public and private debt.

One of my Perth clients was no exception. We started working together when times were good. There were high profile projects, many exciting opportunities to grow and a seemingly sensible path for them to become an industry leader. We focussed on building a strong Profit per X (single economic denominator from Jim Collins book *'Good to Great: Why Some Companies Make the Leap...and Others Don't'*), a powerful Brand Promise and meaningful Core Purpose (from the same book). The intersection of these three areas is what Jim Collins calls the Hedgehog concept and is discussed later in section 4.5 of this book.

Also, we focussed on disciplines within the business, one of which was building up the Core Capital Target – a principle from Greg Crabtree of having two months of fixed expenses as spare cash in a separate bank account.

You know, just in case.

Then the downturn hit.

Industry revenues declined by 70% in one year.

Every month when we would meet he would explain how yet another competitor had collapsed and how there were more companies competing over the same projects and the rates just kept dropping.

I think it was a combination of luck and timing to introduce these disciplines.

We were lucky that we had implemented the Core Capital Target and had enough cash in the bank to run the business for two months without revenue if needed. That gave us a buffer to not panic and think strategically.

We were lucky that we had validated the key components of our strategy, and when we saw that we were unable to sustain the business with the current industry sales, we identified actions to generate new revenue streams in areas that were not affected by the mining downturn, yet would align with our Core Purpose, enable us to deliver on our Brand Promise to customers and improve our Profit per X, our single economic denominator.

We were lucky that we had established the habit of a meeting rhythm to go offsite for a full day every 90 days and work on the business, to undertake strategic thinking and build an execution plan with clear priorities for the coming quarter.

An industry downturn is a bit like placing a frog in a pot, then placing it over a flame, where the water temperature gradually increases until it is boiling and the frog dies.

Unless you can step out of the day to day and go 'offsite' to think strategically, ideally with an external coach who understands your business, you are at risk of not taking action until it is too late.

For my client over the course of that year we took the single original revenue stream and over time developed six new revenue streams each within a new division. Today, a few years later, each of these new revenue streams is unaffected by mining downturns, all have a Profit per X between two and three times the original division and the forecast revenues for each of the six new divisions are greater than the original division revenues.

Tool

The most important part of the offsite planning is the first part. That is actually booking in the meetings and holding them. Of course the structure of reflection and accountability, strategic thinking and execution planning are vitally important, but for most people, just booking four, quarterly offsite dates in their calendar is often one of the most important steps.

I would go as far as to say that even if a leadership team went offsite together and just chatted all day, four times, 90 days apart in a year, in a completely undisciplined manner, instead of just going to the office as they normally do, it would still have a positive impact on the company.

First, ensure that you have dates booked in your calendar for one year ahead for all leadership team members. My recommendation is one, two-day annual workshop to build an annual plan along with the first 90-day plan, and three, one day quarterly workshops per year each to build a 90-day plan. Then on the months without a quarterly or annual workshop, you would hold half day monthly meetings to deep dive on the progress of priorities, and course correct as required.

Next, once you have set the dates and your team is holding regular, disciplined meetings, the real challenge – and opportunity – emerges. That is aligning your company's rhythms and activities with the meeting rhythms. For example, having the discipline to update staff on a topic at a daily or weekly meeting, rather than an email to all. Or only asking for an update to an important project at a weekly meeting instead of whenever the idea pops into your head throughout the week. Holding the meetings is one thing, aligning your people with this discipline is where the real value in the meeting rhythm comes from. The simple question to ask yourself in between daily or weekly meetings before you communicate

Meeting rhythm planner

	MONTHLY EXECUTION PROGRESS HALF DAY PER MONTH E.G. 14TH DAY OF JAN, FEB, APR, MAY, JUL, AUG, OCT, NOV	QUARTERLY QUARTERLY PRIORITIES 1 DAY PER QUARTER E.G. MAR 14, SEPT 14, DEC 14	ANNUAL STRATEGIC THINKING 2 DAYS PER YEAR E.G. JUN 14 & 15
January			
February			
March			
April			
May			
June			
July			
August			
September			
October			
November			
December			

should be 'Is the status update or enquiry I'm about to communicate a part of the agenda for our daily or weekly meeting?'. If is it, then wait.

Generally an agenda for your offsite workshop should begin with reflection on the past quarter or year for the first few hours with each team member reporting final updates and closing off the past quarters KPIs and priorities from the last planning session. Then time should be spent on strategic thinking, with the amount of time relative to whether it's a quarterly or annual workshop and finally the last few hours should be dedicated to execution planning, developing the three to five priorities for the next 90 days for the company and each department.

More specifically the objective of an annual planning offsite workshop is to undertake valuable strategic thinking. The type of in depth thinking to identify what the organisation must do in order to achieve a unique and valuable position in the market within a three-year timeframe and evolve the work that has already been done. This is in contrast to the quarterly workshop which is to set 90-day priorities which align with the strategy and the monthly meeting which is to monitor the metrics as well as track and adjust the progress of the 90-day priorities.

For a detailed explanation of the quarterly and annual meeting rhythm, refer to the book *Scaling Up* by Verne Harnish.

Set your planning meeting dates now.

Key points

★ Strategic thinking is the process to evolve the central ideas within your strategy over time.

★ Execution planning is the process of determining the priorities and goals that will progress toward your strategy in the next 90 days.

★ This process is best undertaken within a structured meeting rhythm, and facilitated by an external coach.

Key Resources

★ *Jack: Straight from the Gut* - Jack Welch

★ 'Corporate Strategists under fire' - Fortune Magazine 1982 - Walter Kiechel

★ "What is Strategy" - Harvard Business Review - Michael Porter - https://hbr.org/1996/11/what-is-strategy

★ *Good to Great: Why Some Companies Make the Leap...and Others Don't* - Jim Collins

★ *Simple Numbers, Straight Talk, Big Profits!: 4 Keys to Unlock Your Business Potential* - Core Capital Target - Greg Crabtree

★ *Scaling Up: How a Few Companies Make It...and Why the Rest Don't* (Rockefeller Habits 2.0) - Verne Harnish

4.2 The company's long term 10+ year BHAG® is known by all staff and actions are taken each quarter to progress toward the BHAG®

Principle

The phrase Big Hairy Audacious Goal or BHAG® was developed by Jim Collins and Jerry Porras in their book *Built to Last: Successful Habits of Visionary Companies*. The BHAG® is a 10- to 30-year goal that reinforces the business fundamentals and challenges the company to greatness.

The BHAG® represents a far off destination, a North Star the company is aiming for over a long period of time and should be considered a natural outcome from the success of the strategy within the aforementioned time frame. By their very definition, a BHAG® needs to be big and audacious, and in my experience, people dramatically underestimate what they can achieve in 10 years and dramatically overestimate what they can achieve in 90 days.

So why do we need a BHAG®, and why is it so important that all staff know the BHAG®?

As further detailed in section 4.5 of this book, the BHAG® is discovered by firstly developing a deep understanding of the 3 elements of the hedgehog, being, a company's Core Purpose, its Profit per X and its Brand Promise. Then one considers, with the relentless pursuit of these three elements over a ten to thirty-year timeframe, where could the company go?

What could the company achieve?

The hedgehog concept and the resultant BHAG® are useful to maintaining discipline within an organisation for two reasons.

It provides a simple tool for decision makers to consistently maintain the discipline of the long term company strategy as outlined in section 4.5 of this book. When faced with a decision to make, this tool answers at a basic level the question 'should we do this, does this align with our hedgehog?'

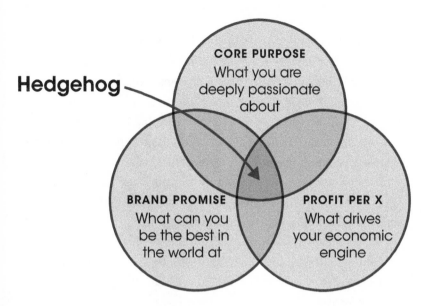

Hedgehog

CORE PURPOSE
What you are
deeply passionate
about

BRAND PROMISE
What can you
be the best in
the world at

PROFIT PER X
What drives
your economic
engine

The hedgehog concept adapted from Jim Collins

It provides a simple question for leaders to ask through the rhythm of quarterly and annual strategic thinking. When attending a quarterly or annual meeting it creates the question 'what actions should we take in the next year or quarter to move the needle toward our BHAG®?'

And that second point is literally how simple it is within the structured discipline of a strategic thinking meeting rhythm. Every quarter asking three key questions to the leadership team.

What do we need to do in order to live our Core Purpose in the next 90 days which will move the needle to ultimately achieve our BHAG®?

What do we need to do in order to improve our Profit per X in the next 90 days which will move the needle to ultimately achieve our BHAG®?

What do we need to do relating to our Brand Promise in the next 90 days which will move the needle to ultimately achieve our BHAG®?

As the old saying goes, if you don't know where you are going, any road will take you there.

Not all companies share a vision, or even a plan. In fact, according to research by the UK's department of Business Innovation and Skills (BIS), 32% of employees doubt their company has a plan at all!

You can't build a great company without great people, and great people have a deep-seated desire to understand why they commit their efforts to a company, to what end their creative energies are contributing to a goal, where the company they are working for wants to go, and what part of that goal they are working on.

To have everyone understand the BHAG® is to have everyone aligned in understanding the CEOs vision for the company, and the more important the vision, the easier it will be to attract the best people to work for you.

If your dream is to put a ding in the universe, as Steve Jobs said, or to make the world more open and connected, as Mark Zuckerberg said, it will be easier to attract the best talent.

However, if you don't have a vision that is inspiring, something big and cool you are trying to achieve that 'could' potentially get your lowest paid employee out of bed on a cold winter's morning, you are just another business. By creating just another business, you are going to end up with employees who just want a job.

And the problem with employees who just want a job is that they are less engaged, or potentially actively disengaged compared with those who believe in, and want to help you achieve your Big Hairy Audacious Goal.

Of course, once you have chosen your BHAG®, you can't just leave it in a desk drawer or on a foyer wall. You need to bring it to life. Everyone needs to know it and you need to make sure that the day to day activities that people are working on align with, and contribute to the achievement of this long term goal.

Story

Kevin operates an IT firm with around $22 million in revenues and 80 staff servicing medium-sized businesses across the country. Like many IT services firms the world over, during the past ten years he has been focussed on evolving from a company selling computers and technician hours to a company selling managed services contracts, or selling contracts with a fixed monthly cost per user, whereby all computer maintenance on a customers site is covered.

A part of this evolution from a project and break / fix company to a company managing IT contracts is Kevin's Profit per X, or single economic denominator. This focus is to win more managed services contracts, with a higher Gross Profit. Therefore, the Profit per X is Gross Profit per client under contract.

The company has a relentless focus on winning more contracts and improving the gross profit within each contract.

Also, the company is passionate about customer happiness, and use the Net Promoter Score (NPS), a measure of customer satisfaction, to survey the likelihood of a customer recommending them.

For Kevin, the BHAG® became $100 million in revenue under contract in ten years with a NPS score greater than 70.

To put the NPS score into context, Apple worldwide has a NPS of 72, and according to Customer Monitor, one of the leading NPS software providers, across Australia the average IT services company has a minus-2 score. So not only is the jump in revenues a challenge, 70 is indeed Big and Audacious!

In order to bring the BHAG® to life, and to align people and priorities behind it, Kevin has painted a huge mural of a mountain in their boardroom with three paths leading to the summit. One path is the revenue path with a goal of $100 million under contract, the second is a Gross Profit target with a goal of 70% and the third is a NPS target with the goal of 70. Each month when the results are published the three BHAG® results are posted on the wall in the corresponding section of the BHAG® mountain.

Adjacent the BHAG® mountain is the list of priorities that the company is working on each quarter to progress toward the BHAG®.

Then at the company offsite planning workshop the leadership team knows how they are tracking toward the BHAG®. Here they can answer the crucial question, "What do we need to do in the next quarter to get closer to achieving our BHAG®?" Many of the company priorities, either at a company-wide or department level come from the discipline this produces.

Employees have a similar mural of the mountain at their desk which is designed to remind them not only of the BHAG®, but instead of the company wide goals of revenue under contract, Gross Profit and NPS, it tracks their department metrics and the priorities for their department.

Everyone knows what the company goals are, how they are progressing toward those goals and the priorities they are working on currently to achieve these long-term goals. Knowing the long term goals aligns people behind the short term goals at a company wide and department level.

Tool

Maybe posters of mountains aren't your thing. That's okay. Your objective is to understand best practice, and how to make best practice work best in your business.

Once you have decided upon your BHAG® the value comes from maintaining a discipline on the Core Purpose, Profit per X and Brand Promise, every single quarter for many years. Also, the value comes from having alignment within your team, having everyone focussed on creating priorities which align with the BHAG® for the company and each department.

If you have a multiple part BHAG®, as Kevin did with three parts, you will need to track the progress of each part. Then for each part, along with the Core Purpose, Profit per X and Brand Promise, ask the question what do we need to do in the next quarter to achieve these as outlined in the table below.

Quarterly hedgehog assessment

	WHAT WE NEED TO DO IN THE NEXT 90 DAYS TO MOVE THE NEEDLE TOWARD OUR BHAG®?
CORE PURPOSE	
BRAND PROMISE	
PROFIT PER X	

If you have a 5-part BHAG® it might look like this

Quarterly hedgehog assessment

	WHAT WE NEED TO DO IN THE NEXT 90 DAYS TO MOVE THE NEEDLE TOWARD OUR BHAG®?
CORE PURPOSE	
BRAND PROMISE	
PROFIT PER X	
PART 3	
PART 4	
PART 5	

Every quarter use your strategic thinking time at quarterly offsite workshops to interpret your advancement toward the BHAG® and set priorities for both the company and departments to advance further by responding to these questions.

Key points

★ It's important to have all staff understand the objective and long term goal of the company.

★ The BHAG® is the ten to thirty year goal of the company and is developed from a deep understanding of what the company is passionate about, what drives the economic engine and what the company can be the best at.

★ At each quarterly offsite the leadership team should review the BHAG® progress and plan relevant actions.

Key Resources

★ *Built to Last: Successful Habits of Visionary Companies* - Jim Collins and Jerry I. Porras

4.3 Ideal Customer needs are identified and the Brand Promise is helping to attract the best customers in the market

Principle

If you try to be everything to everyone, you end up being nothing to no one.

Or as Sally Hogshead more elegantly said in her book *Fascinate: How to Make Your Brand Impossible to Resist* 'If you're not eliciting a negative response from someone, then you're probably not very compelling to anyone.' If you are trying to please everyone, you'll likely not resonate with anyone.

The famous strategist Michael Porter tells us in his book *Competitive Advantage: Creating and sustaining superior performance* that there are three ways to achieve above average performance in an industry:

★ Serve the many needs of a few customers
★ Serve the unique needs of many customers
★ Serve many needs for many customers in a specific segment of the market

Therefore, achieving a unique and valuable position in the market where you outperform competitors initially requires that you complete three things:

1. Gain a deep understanding of your Core Competencies, the unique combination of systems and processes your company has developed over the years which indicate what you are capable of being great at

2. Assess your market, and determine where no one else is excelling, know where you can deliver activities better than any other organisation and no others are focussed

3. After the above two items, consider Porter's three customer needs above and determine who is the customer that you would need to serve in order to successfully become great, and what are their needs

As Shannon Susko said in her book 3*HAG Way: The Strategic Execution System that ensures your strategy is not a Wild-Ass-Guess!,* 'You're not competing directly against your competitors, you're competing to be unique in the marketplace'.

That should be the ultimate goal of your strategic planning process. To become unique and valuable in the marketplace.

In every business, in every market, there are customers who are better and those who are worse. I'm certain that you could easily list the customers who you would never deal with again if given the chance, and also the ones you would love to replicate if it were possible.

The customer isn't always right. Instead giving the best customers what they need is what is right. It takes courage to deliver something that you know will upset some customers, whilst delighting others.

For Apple, the ideal customer in the 1990s was a creative individual to whom beautiful design mattered, who was prepared to pay more for a computer that had software designed to make creative pursuits easier.

There is no doubt that Apple has the courage to upset customers, and it seems every time they release a new product they develop more and more courage, and upset more people such as their 2016 'innovations' with the removal of the headphone jack from the iPhone and the removal of all useful ports such as USB-A, MagSafe, HDMI and Thunderbolt from the MacBook Pro in lieu of only USB-C ports.

Unfortunately, this upset many Apple customers as most used these ports daily.

Over the years it can be argued that Apple has evolved to become more of a luxury brand, perhaps a status symbol for its users. In his book

The Four: The Hidden DNA of Amazon, Apple, Facebook, and Google, Scott Galloway demonstrates the correlation between average household income and iPhone ownership across U.S. cities and shows how today Apple should be classed as a luxury brand and not a tech company.

Within the smartphone market in Q1 2017, Apple's iOS iPhone Operating System represented a mere 13.7% of sales, yet in the same period accounted for 83% of the industry profits. For smartphone manufacturers to whom profit matters, Apple probably has the best and most loyal customers. By evolving into a luxury technology brand, an area where no others play, Apple owns the high end luxury phone market, and along with it most of the profit in the entire industry.

The challenge is to find the customer need that is untapped in your industry, where you can access a greater profit by meeting the customers needs better than anyone else. Therefore, you need to know who your ideal customer is, what their needs are and relentlessly deliver on this.

Story

It always amuses me when I see an electrical or plumbing van on the road and emblazoned across the side it says "Specialising in" and they go on to list every type of work they could ever have possibly done. Houses, offices, factories and the list goes on. By simple definition of the word specialise, it's not possible to specialise in every single type of work you could possibly do!

GA PERRY, a 122-year-old plumbing and electrical business based in Perth specialise in one thing: being on time. Their Brand Promise is that they will 'be on time or it's free'.

The GA PERRY ideal customer is a busy person who is prepared to pay more to have an electrician or plumber meet at their home at the planned time. All of the systems, processes and people within GA PERRY have evolved over many years to support this Brand Promise and delivering this Brand Promise is at the centre of their business model and strategy.

Says Alvin Mckavanagh, GA PERRY Managing Director, 'I felt that meant we had to ensure our call centre/operations centre needed to run logistically, no differently to a one hour delivery courier company. However, the next challenge was getting everyone on board to running logistically, requiring continual communication between the office and field staff every 30 minutes for updates.'

GA PERRY evolved their operational excellence to consistently deliver this Brand Promise. They have systems and back up systems to ensure that their tradespeople arrive at the designated time as no one wants to be responsible for the call that was late and that wasn't paid for.

GA PERRY have built a unique and valuable position in the market by undertaking a different set of activities from competitors.

It hasn't been easy by any means to build this position. It has taken many years of development around this central idea as well as marketing and building the brand. But when it comes to their relentless focus on delivering their Brand Promise to their ideal customer, GA PERRY understands who their ideal customer is. They also understand what their ideal customer needs, and by constantly delivering on that Brand Promise, they are attracting the best customers in the market.

Tool

As Jim Collins said in his book *Good to Great: Why Some Companies Make the Leap...and Others Don't*, 'doing what you are good at will only make you good; focusing solely on what you can potentially do better than any other organisation is the only path to greatness'. As Collins goes on to say, 'good is the enemy of great'.

You aren't going to build a great business that attracts the best customers in the market if you focus on what you can only be good at. Instead, you must have a deep understanding of what you can truly be great at.

Think about your business in the long term, the ten-year timeframe. Make a list of things that you can only be good at within that timeframe, and a second list of things you can do better than any other organisation. Be brutally honest, and ensure you keep your ego in check.

Remember GA PERRY could only be as good as the other good plumbers and electricians in their market: a power point installed in a home is the same as any other. However, they could be better than anyone else at being on time, and that really mattered to a profitable niche of customers!

Good to best comparison

THINGS WE CAN ONLY BE GOOD AT	THINGS WE CAN DO BETTER THAN ANY OTHER ORGANISATION

Once you understand the things that you can do better than any other organisation, and I acknowledge, it's a tough list to write, begin to think about your ideal customer and how the things you can do better than any other organisation align with the needs of the ideal customer.

In order to determine the needs of the ideal customer, first who is your ideal customer? Select five real customers in your business that you would like to replicate if given the chance and write the single characteristic of that client that caused you to select them.

Ideal customer characteristics

REAL CUSTOMER NAME	CHARACTERISTIC (E.G. PAYS ON TIME, GIVES US ALL THEIR BUSINESS ETC)
1.	
2.	
3.	
4.	
5.	

Now that you have the characteristics of five clients you would love to replicate, combine them into a single, virtual, ideal customer and give this customer a name. For example you might have 'Rob, a technical professional who pays on time, gives us all their business and is organised'. Write this in the table below adjacent 'Our Ideal Customer'.

In the table below, consider the top five needs of your ideal customer. Ensure this is the needs and not wants of the ideal customer, as a customer can want, want, want you into bankruptcy.

Ideal customer needs

Need 1	
Need 2	
Need 3	
Need 4	
Need 5	

Next consider the interdependency between what your ideal customer needs, and what your organisation can do better than anyone else. If you were to focus on what you can do better than any other organisation in a 3 year timeframe, whilst delivering on your ideal customers needs, what three things can you promise to your customers that are unique and measurable? Write these below.

Brand promises

Brand Promise 1	
Brand Promise 2	
Brand Promise 3	

If you were to relentlessly focus on the things you can do better than any other organisation, your Brand Promises, the items that align with your ideal customers needs, and you developed your systems, processes and people to align with this each quarter over three years, what would you need to stop doing in order to focus on this?

Make a list of the things your organisation must stop doing in order to focus on the things you can do better than any other organisation.

Stop list to focus on the Brand Promises

THINGS TO STOP DOING IN ORDER TO FOCUS ON WHAT YOU CAN DO BETTER THAN ANY OTHER ORGANISATION

1	
2	
3	
4	
5	

Over time, the intent is to use the resources freed up by stopping the things you can only be good at and channelling the those resources toward the things you can do better than any other organisation. Your job then is to have these things you can do better evolve into your Brand Promise and for your organisation to become the best at consistently delivering on these promises.

Once you understand what you can do better than any other organisation, that meets the needs of your ideal customer, you can develop a unique and measurable Brand Promise that will attract the best customers in the market.

Finally remember from the culture section of this book that your goal is to bridge the gap between ideal employees and ideal customers, with the organisation living its Core Purpose as outlined in the diagram below. The Brand Promise describes *how* you will deliver your why (Core Purpose) to your who (ideal customer).

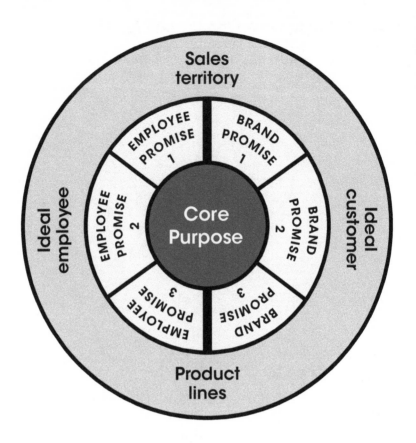

Key points

★ An Ideal Customer represents the person who will pay the most profit and obtain the most value from your organisation.

★ Understanding their needs and how you can uniquely meet those needs is a key element of strategy.

★ This should culminate in a Brand Promise, a unique and measurable statement which attracts and converts the best customers.

Key Resources

★ *Fascinate: How to Make Your Brand Impossible to Resist* - Sally Hogshead

★ *Competitive Advantage: Creating and sustaining superior performance* - Michael Porter

★ *3HAG Way: The Strategic Execution System that ensures your strategy is not a Wild-Ass-Guess!* - Shannon Susko

★ *The Four: The Hidden DNA of Amazon, Apple, Facebook, and Google* - Scott Galloway

★ *Good to Great: Why Some Companies Make the Leap... and Others Don't* - Jim Collins

4.4 Brand Promise KPIs are measured weekly and performance is displayed all around the business

Principle

Earlier in this chapter I outlined the statistic from Walter Kiechel of Harvard Business School that 90% of strategies fail due to poor execution. If your company's Brand Promise is a central part of your strategy, it is your job to bring it to life through good execution.

In his book *Mastering the Rockefeller Habits: What You Must Do to Increase the Value of Your Fast Growth Firm*, Verne Harnish outlined the three disciplines that lead to good execution:

PRIORITIES - having everyone in the organisation knowing the top 3 to 5 priorities for the company, department and each individual

METRICS / DATA - having the right data to make the right decisions at the right time

MEETING RHYTHM - having a regular rhythm of daily / weekly / monthly / quarterly meetings to improve communication and increase the pulse of the business decision making

If we consider how to execute the Brand Promise in this context, we have:

PRIORITIES - have everyone in the business know that the Brand Promise is a priority because it is displayed all around the business on posters and dashboards

METRICS - dashboards throughout the business are displaying Brand Promise KPIs

MEETING RHYTHM - at each weekly meeting for the leadership team the latest results from the Brand Promise KPIs are updated and discussed

This is a system to implement that will align the activities of your business with the needs of your ideal customers. Remember that a Brand Promise isn't a tagline; it is *how* you will sell your *'what'* to your *'who'*, and it results in revenues organically coming to your business. Customers want to buy from you because you meet their needs better than anyone else, and you are better at it than any other organisation.

But this system must be maintained. It is like brushing your teeth. It's not a once-in-a-while thing – it's an all-the-time thing. Your goal is to try and avoid the credibility chasm, that is the difference between what you say (your Brand Promise) and what you do in the eyes of your customer.

If your Brand Promise is displayed all around the business, and the results are discussed each week, salespeople and customer facing employees can use it as a legitimate and authentic tool with customers.

For example, if your Brand Promise was that you will respond to customer requests in 1 hour, when making that statement to a customer, a sales person could say 'and in the past week we have had 1,500 customer requests with 96% responded to in one hour'. So not only does the Brand Promise deliver on the customers need thereby driving revenues to your business, by measuring it weekly and bringing it to life it helps salespeople build trust and close sales easier.

Story

Adam operates a construction business. The first time we mapped out the ideal customer needs a few years ago we identified that the most important thing to the ideal customer was to deliver a project on time. That is, in the construction project plan a final delivery date was assigned, and the most important thing was that this date was met.

We evaluated Adam's performance against this, and the leadership team rated their performance a 3/5, not awful, not great. We then ranked two of the main competitors and both rated a 4/5, significantly better than us! We had identified that we believed for the thing that matters the most to the ideal customer, delivering on time, that the company's two main competitors were consistently delivering on time around 20% better than we were!

From that discussion, the Brand Promise was developed to be On time, First Time, Every time. Adam stuck the phrase in enormous 6-inch letters on the wall in his office and began to measure the number of projects that were on time the first time – meaning that they were fully complete and didn't need to postpone the completion date. In the building foyer a large screen was installed which tracked the Brand Promise KPIs.

Upon further investigation we learned that one of the main things that contributed to not delivering on time the first time was 'go backs', having to go back and repair or rectify work that wasn't installed correctly.

The systems and processes to overview and check completed works were improved and ownership of this certification given to staff members. Importantly the cost of these 'go backs' was also tracked and has now saved the company well over $2 million in the past couple of years.

Tool

By definition your Brand Promise must be measurable.

The difficult part is that you probably aren't measuring your Brand Promise KPIs when you set them. In my experience as a coach having helped developed hundreds of Brand Promise KPIs, there are two types of KPIs to avoid.

First, avoid KPIs that are right but will take an enormous amount of effort to capture. For Adam building the systems to display the projects that were delivered on time on a screen in the foyer took time and resources. But he could have started with a whiteboard on the wall. It's not an unreasonable question to ask each week how many projects did we finish this week and how many were delivered on time? The KPIs were easy to measure.

Second, try to avoid KPIs that can only be measured very rarely. This can be a bit more difficult. I work with a business in the Christmas decoration industry with an annual sales and delivery cycle. For them it is really difficult to avoid KPIs that are rarely measured. Everything happens on an annual basis!

The reason that measuring Brand Promise KPIs on a weekly basis is prescribed is that it helps you to pulse faster. It might seem easier to produce the Brand Promise KPIs within the monthly reports but weekly reports help you to make micro changes on a regular basis that over time provide a large impact. By measuring these KPIs weekly, Adam said he had developed a two-to-four week advantage over his competitors who were only reporting in the middle of the following month, after accounting was complete and the books were closed.

Having beautiful, dynamic dashboards is nice, and might be something to aim for, but a meaningful way to commence might be developing the habit of writing the Brand Promise KPIs on a whiteboard at a weekly team meeting to begin with.

Using the simple table on the following page you can track each of your weekly Brand Promise KPIs throughout the quarter.

Quarterly Brand Promise dashboard

	BRAND PROMISE 1	BRAND PROMISE 2	BRAND PROMISE 3
WEEKLY TARGET GREEN / RED			
WEEK 1			
WEEK 2			
WEEK 3			
WEEK 4			
WEEK 5			
WEEK 6			
WEEK 7			
WEEK 8			
WEEK 9			
WEEK 10			
WEEK 11			
WEEK 12			
WEEK 13			

Key points

★ By definition Brand Promises must be measurable.

★ Displaying your Brand Promise KPIs all around the business and discussing the results each week enables salespeople and customer facing employees to both be aware of it and use it with customers.

Key Resources

★ *Mastering the Rockefeller Habits: What You Must Do to Increase the Value of Your Fast Growth Firm* - Verne Harnish

4.5 Each key product or service contributes to the company hedgehog and any which do not are discontinued

Principle

The term hedgehog in our context comes from Jim Collins book *Good to Great: Why Some Companies Make the Leap...and Others Don't,* and is originally from the Greek poet Archilochus, who said 'The fox knows many things, but the hedgehog knows one big thing'. This can be interpreted that the fox, for all his cunning, is defeated by the hedgehog's one defence.

From Jim Collins: 'Whereas a fox will pursue many ends at the same time, and see the world in all its complexity, the hedgehog simplifies a complex world into a single organising idea, a basic principle or concept that unifies and guides everything... reducing all challenges and dilemmas to a simple hedgehog idea'.

The hedgehog concept is found at the intersection of three circles and is more than a strategy. It's really an understanding about how to maintain discipline.

These three circles are;

What are you deeply passionate about? Your Core Purpose, the reason beyond profit that your company exists.

What drives your economic engine? Your Profit per X, the single metric that has the greatest impact on your economics, that your company relentlessly pursues.

What can you be the best in the world at? Your Brand Promise, the unique promise you make that meets your ideal customers need.

At the centre is your hedgehog. A simple and clear principle that prescribes what to maintain discipline on over the long term.

Jim Collins research identifies that by maintaining discipline on the hedgehog over a long period, this discipline and focus will help achieve the BHAG® or Big Hairy Audacious Goal.

The problem I have observed is that people in leadership teams set a 10- to 30-year BHAG® and obsess over it, oftentimes sacrificing the discipline of the hedgehog and making short term decisions driven by blind faith worshipping the BHAG®. They do not maintain a conscious choice or adherence to discipline on what they must do and what they must not do over the duration of time towards the BHAG® by relentlessly focussing on the hedgehog. They are not consistent.

As Jim Collins said ten years later in his book with Morten Hansen *Great by Choice: Uncertainty, Chaos, and Luck–Why Some Thrive Despite Them All–* 'In a great twist of irony, those who bring about the most significant change in the world, those who have the largest impact on the economy and society, are themselves enormously consistent in their approach'.

A BHAG® is not built by picking a cool sounding, large number that inspires you, it is built by first gaining a deep understanding of the three elements of your hedgehog, the three elements that reinforce the business fundamentals. As mentioned earlier firstly the Core Purpose, second, the single metric that has the greatest impact on your economics and third, what your company can be better at than any other organisation. Only after gaining a deep understanding of the hedgehog do you begin to envisage where the focus might take you if you were to focus on it for a 10- to 30-year period. Not three years, not five years but ten to thirty years of relentless focus and discipline driving toward the intersection of the three circles of your company's Core Purpose, your Profit per X and your Brand Promise. If you executed on that relentless focus and discipline where would you end up? That's the place your BHAG® is discovered.

Of course discovering your BHAG® has no relevance to actually achieving it. Once you discover your BHAG®, what really matters is not the destination, but the disciplined, consistent journey you take, and the focus to get there. That's why it's not about the BHAG®, it's about the hedgehog. The BHAG® might tell you where you are going, but the hedgehog tells you how to get there. The BHAG® is the equivalent to a

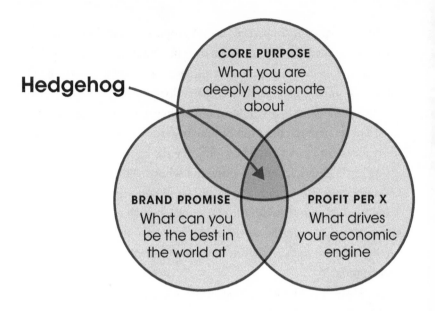

Hedgehog

CORE PURPOSE
What you are
deeply passionate
about

BRAND PROMISE
What can you
be the best in
the world at

PROFIT PER X
What drives
your economic
engine

blank piece of paper with 'point B' written on it, whereas the hedgehog is equivalent to a map which has written on it 'point A', 'point B' and the roads between the two showing how to get there.

How?

What if every time you made a major decision, every time you wanted to open a new office, launch a new product or begin a new initiative there was a simple tool that you could use to validate that decision? What if all the decisions you made were in the same direction, which was the right direction? That is how the hedgehog is used as a filtering tool.

If the BHAG® is the destination you're aiming for, the hedgehog is the compass. Don't rely on the destination to figure out how to reach the destination, rely on the compass all the time.

A good strategy will clearly tell you what to say no to. Without a good strategy, you are likely to take up every opportunity as it arises, creating expensive distraction for you and your team. By easily and quickly knowing when to say no to opportunities and distractions you can get back to executing your strategy. Equally problematic, you might be wasting effort and energy on delivering and maintaining current products and services to clients that don't align with your long term strategy.

But saying no, especially saying it is time to drop a product or service that may be currently contributing revenue and profit takes courage. As with many things in life it's good to ask yourself, do I want to experience pain now, or experience the pain later?

The pain you produce by dropping products and services that don't align with your hedgehog may be significant now, but be confident that in the long run, the pain you may experience by failing to maintain discipline within your hedgehog will cause a lot more pain.

As martial artist and actor Bruce Lee famously said, 'I fear not the man who has practiced 10,000 kicks once, but I fear the man who has practiced one kick 10,000 times'. That 'one kick' should be your hedgehog.

Story

Following on from successful growth as CEO of audio and gaming headphone manufacturer Skull Candy, in 2014 Jeremy Andrus took on the CEO role at Traeger Grills, one of the leading U.S. manufacturers of barbeque grills. Founded by Joe Traeger in 1987 the patented Traeger Pellet Grill feeds compressed wood pellets into a burn pot that indirectly heats and smokes food at a temperature you control.

Now taking on this role came with a unique set of challenges because Traeger isn't your average product manufacturer, it has a deeply loyal following with 75% of owners having influenced the sale of one or more grills, and 25% of owners having influenced the sale of 3 or more grills. If that level of loyalty isn't enough, many customers wear the firm's logo as tattoos!

As a family owned and run business, Traeger had grown for decades on the patented pellet feeder system using compressed sawdust pellets to fuel the grill rather than the standard timber or gas fuel used by traditional barbeque manufacturers. But in 2006, Traeger's patent expired and over the following seven years other manufacturers started to release their own pellet feed grills thereby eating into Traeger's unique market share.

When Jeremy Andrus joined in 2014 as part of an acquisition in conjunction with private-equity firm Trilantic Capital Partners, it was a very different life from his time at Skull Candy. While the support from customers was remarkable, several things the business had previously done were not aligned with the direction the company needed to take in order to achieve their long term goal to achieve $1 billion in revenues, and he realised the company needed to stop doing several things in order to focus on the company's strategic direction.

First he stopped selling through channels that didn't align with the long term strategy.

Says Andrus: 'My first trade show happened two and a-half weeks into my time at Traeger. I showed up with my marketing VP, his first day on the job. I got a bruise on my chest from retailers poking me and telling how bad we were. We had two people with cell phones and laptops managing 1,000 accounts. We had quality issues with the product. We had 42 company stores that were undercutting dealers. We were selling the same product in Costco at a 30% discount to specialty retailers. There was all this channel conflict. It was an interesting dichotomy between consumers who loved us and channel partners who hated us. The original strategy was to grow from 42 stores to 300 stores. As soon as we bought the business, I shut them all down.'

Second, while other manufacturers were focussed on selling a barbeque, or having a Profit per X of Profit per customer, Trager knew that a grill might sell for $500, but if that client also bought the pellet fuel along with sauces and rubs, critical for any serious barbeque pit master, that same customer value was actually over $3,000 through the life of the grill.

Traeger stopped focussing on trying to achieve a better profit per customer sale and instead focussed on profit per repeat customer. The objective was to increase repeat sales, rather than solely focus on one off sales and so Traeger released rubs, sauces and apparel to increase repeat customer purchases.

Third the company stopped building products to a price, and focussed entirely on quality. This led Traeger to heavily invest in product development, in fact to invest more than the company had done in the previous 30 years. The first major new product from this initiative was the release of the Timberline range of grills in April 2017, a $1,700 Internet connected grill that includes recipes on a smartphone app and a level of build quality that was as good as, if not better than any other.

By having the courage to discontinue products and services that didn't align with Traegers hedgehog, Jeremy Andrus provided a strategic focus that has driven revenues from $70 million when he joined in 2014 to over $300 million in 2017, with a 50% growth rate each year and a goal to reach $1 billion revenue.

Tool

In order to maintain the discipline of the hedgehog, its review and consideration when making major decisions must become a habit.

At every strategic planning workshop I facilitate, we review a hedgehog poster, which is on the wall, noting that all major decisions we make in the business must align with the hedgehog. These decisions must pass through the hedgehog filter test whereby we say yes to all three questions.

1. Will saying yes to this help us live our Purpose?

2. Will saying yes to this help us to deliver on our Brand Promise?

3. Will saying yes to this help us improve our Profit per X?

If we can't answer yes to all three of these questions then it doesn't align with our hedgehog and we should not do it. It's not difficult, and may seem monotonous after 10 quarters, but it's importance should not be underestimated.

As Jim Collins says 'The exact same world that had become so simple and clear to the good-to-great companies, remained complex and shrouded in the mist for the comparison companies. For all their change programs, frantic gesticulations, and charismatic leaders – they rarely emerged from the fog ... setting their goals and strategies more from bravado than from understanding'.

And it is this understanding, this deep appreciation for the need to only make changes that align with this simple and clear direction over a long period of time that enables growth and momentum.

How do your products and services align with your hedgehog?

This simple assessment will help you to consider each of your key products or services and how they align with your Purpose, Brand Promise and Profit per X.

Simply rate each of your products and services from 1 to 5.

If you are scoring lower than a 4 out of 5 on any of these criteria, you should seriously consider stopping the sale of this item, now or at some clear date in the future.

It's easy to make excuses and say things like it's a loss leader, or you are worried about how you would deal without those revenues, but if this product or service doesn't help you live your Core Purpose, deliver on your Brand Promise and improve your Profit per X, are you getting the best return on your effort? What if you put that effort into something that did, something you can truly be great at, instead of only good, something that you love doing and at the same time drives your economic engine?

Hedgehog test

	WILL THIS HELP US TO LIVE OUR CORE PURPOSE?	WILL THIS HELP US TO DELIVER ON OUR BRAND PROMISE?	WILL THIS HELP US IMPROVE OUR PROFIT PER X?
Example Widgets	*4/5*	*3/5*	*5/5*
Product 1			
Product 2			
Product 3			
Service 1			
Service 2			
Service 3			

Key points

★ A focus on the hedgehog concept through decision making maintains discipline over time.

★ A good strategy will clearly tell you what to say no to.

★ Leaders should regularly assess the alignment between their products and services and their hedgehog and discontinue those which do not contribute.

Key Resources

★ *Good to Great: Why Some Companies Make the Leap...and Others Don't* - Jim Collins

★ *Great by Choice: Uncertainty, Chaos, and Luck: Why Some Thrive Despite Them All* - Jim Collins and Morten Hansen

★ SUCCESSION PLANNING

5.0 Key risks to the business are reduced through succession planning

One of the great frustrations of business is working hard to make a profit one month, only to make a loss the following month. You come out of the two months having neither made nor lost money, only broken even.

Within any business, there is a continual momentum of marketing, the momentum of sales, the momentum of operations and the momentum of finance and administration. Business never stands still.

If two of the five key results of a leader are achieving consistent growth and consistent execution, then reducing the risk within these four business functions of marketing, sales, operations and finance/administration is fundamentally important to maintain that consistency. These risks are best mitigated by succession planning, or having a 'plan B' when something goes wrong, as something so often does.

This chapter outlines how to maintain consistency through people you employ, products and services you sell, suppliers who support you and investment decisions you make. Any lack of consistency through these areas will have an impact on the consistency of your growth and execution.

The problem is that succession planning isn't sexy. Building a culture that people love is sexy, executing a strategy that grows revenues at a fast rate is sexy. For some CEOs, being an ambassador and developing an accountability framework is even sexy. But very few CEOs or entrepreneurs think that succession planning is sexy.

But your job isn't meant to be sexy. You are not a catwalk model or a rock star.

You are a leader.

Your job as a leader is to build a great business and the result of your efforts will be a higher percentage of top performers with a higher retention rate, higher productivity, consistent growth and consistent results.

You could produce the best accountability framework, be an amazing ambassador, win the best places to work awards through your culture efforts and have a strategy growing revenues. But it is all worthless if you can't deliver consistently. Consistent delivery occurs through succession planning, by having a 'plan B'. It's not sexy, but it's important.

A good friend of mine 'coach Kevin' Lawrence of 'Lawrence & Co' advisors from Vancouver, Canada suggests that at its heart, most of the interactions a business coach has with a leadership team and their CEO is about people. It's about people doing the right thing, making the right decisions, understanding how to lead other people and how to get people aligned.

In Kevin's book *Your Oxygen Mask First - 17 Habits to Help High Achievers Survive and Thrive In Life* he reinforces this point and outlines that much of what CEOs and leaders do is interacting with people, and that there is a key responsibility that comes with being a leader: to be on the lookout for dangerous or concerning mental health behaviours. This responsibility arises not only because you need to look after your fellow humans, but because built into the very relationship between a person and their boss is that a boss will push and challenge a person to create results and achieve.

You need to know when to push and challenge, and when to back off. You need to know when to coach a person, when to get external coaching for a person and when to recommend professional help in the form of a therapist or psychologist. Kevin introduced me to the Mental

Mental Health Continuum Model

HEALTHY	REACTING	INJURED	ILL
• Normal mood fluctuations • Calm & takes things in stride • Good sense of humour • Performing well • In control mentally • Normal sleep patterns • Few sleep difficulties • Physically well • Good energy level • Physically and socially active • No or limited alcohol use/ gambling	• Irritable / impatient • Nervous • Sadness / overwhelmed • Displaced sarcasm • Procrastination • Forgetfulness • Trouble sleeping • Intrusive thoughts • Nightmares • Muscle tension / headaches • Low energy • Decreased activity/socializing • Regular but controlled alcohol use / gambling	• Anger • Anxiety • Pervasively sad / hopeless • Negative attitude • Poor performance / workaholic • Poor concentration / decisions • Restless disturbed sleep • Recurrent images / nightmares • Increased aches and pains • Increased fatigue • Avoidance • Withdrawal • Increased alcohol use / gambling is hard to control	• Angry outbursts / aggression • Excessive anxiety / panic attacks • Depressed / suicidal thoughts • Over insubordination • Can't perform duties, control behaviour or concentrate • Can't fall asleep or stay asleep • Sleeping too much or too little • Physical illnesses • Constant fatigue • Not going out or answering phone • Alcohol or gambling addiction • Other addictions

Health Continuum tool from the Canadian Mental Health Commission several years ago and I regularly use it in my coaching with CEOs and leaders, and I further recommend they use it as a go-to tool.

In the people you deal with, consider are their behaviours healthy, reacting, injured or ill?

If you are always pushing your team to achieve, when is too much? What are the early warning signs?

As a leader, if you observe concerning behaviours, what can you do?

When considering your role of succession planning, maintaining consistent results and consistent execution through your business, if you are pushing people to the point where they are not mentally healthy, or other parts of their life are creating mental health issues, they place your goal of consistency at risk.

Or perhaps a better way to put it is unless you look after your people, then you will put your consistency at risk.

What Can Managers Do?

HEALTHY	REACTING	INJURED	ILL

- Lead by example
- Get to know employees
- Foster healthy climate
- Identify and resolve problems early
- Deal with performance issues promptly
- Demonstrate genuine concern
- Provide opportunities for rest
- Advocate

- Watch for behaviour changes
- Adjust workload as required
- Know the resources & how to access them
- Reduce barriers to seeking help
- Encourage early access to care
- Consult with human resources / medical resources as required

- Involve mental health resources
- Respect confidentiality
- Minimize rumours
- Respect medical employment limitations
- Appropriately employ personnel
- Maintain respectful contact
- Involve members in social support
- Seek consultation as needed
- Manage unacceptable behaviours

Key points

★ Succession planning is important to maintain consistent growth and consistent execution.

★ It should include people you employ, products and services you sell, suppliers who support you and investment decisions you make.

★ Leaders should know how to observe the basics that could be a cause for mental health concern, along with when to help, and when to seek help from professionals.

Key Resources

★ *Your Oxygen Mask First - 17 Habits to Help High Achievers Survive and Thrive In Life* - Kevin Lawrence

★ Mental Health Continuum https://www.canada.ca/en/treasury-board-secretariat/services/values-ethics/diversity-equity/disability-management/fundamentals-employers-responsibilities

5.1 Each significant role within the organisation has a virtual bench of at least two people who are contacted quarterly

Principle

Most leaders dislike recruiting with a passion.

They see long and detailed interviews as a waste of time and interviewing people who will not actually get the job as an even greater waste of time.

I know I had a dream about how recruitment should work when I was a young entrepreneur, which I have also identified in many other leaders, and it goes a little something like this.

First, a role becomes vacant, through a resignation, a sacking or simply growth.

As soon as this is identified an advert is placed on an online Job Board such as Monster, Seek or Craigslist.

The very next day a single person applies, and they are both over experienced and overqualified for the role. Also, because the salary paid for the role wasn't disclosed, the person is asking for a salary that is well below the allocated salary. No other candidate applies for the role.

And best of all this single applicant is able to start the very next day.

I put it to you that in all the hundreds of millions of people who have been employed around the world that this dream of so many employers has never happened, not even once. But because this dream is so deeply rooted in the subconscious of so many leaders, they don't do the hiring process justice. Consequently, they end up with mediocre staff.

They spend less time hiring and as a result end up spending a lot more time performance managing and firing. Or at the very least managing mediocrity in their teams.

If you want to build a truly great company, your first step must be to 'get the right people' according to Jim Collins, author of *Good to Great: Why Some Companies Make the Leap...and Others Don't*. Brad Smart, author of *Topgrading: How Leading Companies Win by Hiring, Coaching and Keeping the Best People*, describes the right people as 'A' players, defined as people who are in the top 10 percent of available candidates at the pay rate you are offering. Once employed, these people would be considered as successful hires if they were consistently achieving their Key Performance Indicators and living the Core Values after being employed for one year in the business. They both make the numbers and align with the behavioural expectations of the organisation.

So how do you consistently employ people in the top 10 percent of available candidates at the pay rate you are offering?

Well, first, you must completely let go of the dream of hiring the first and only candidate who is qualified to do the role, to make your life as easy as possible during the hiring process. Instead you must consider yourself as a custodian of the Core Values and productivity of the existing team members and be prepared to go to whatever lengths necessary in order to perform this custodian role. If you make a new hire who isn't a strong cultural fit or doesn't achieve the required numbers that person will damage the culture and your decision will be to blame.

You need to spend more time hiring and less time firing.

This means don't simply place an advert on an online job board and see what turns up. You need to be passionate about uncovering amazing new people, the best people who can make your business a better place to work. One of the keys to this principle from *Topgrading* is the virtual bench, this is a simple process to uncover the A players within the market for a role, well before you would need those people, and to then maintain a virtual bench for every key role.

Imagine a football team who have players on the field who are playing (your current employees), and players who are sitting on the bench at the side of the field waiting on their opportunity to play. This is where the name virtual bench is derived from and the process should allow you to access at least two pre-qualified candidates on top of your other recruiting efforts. And that's the key, the virtual bench should not be your only means to find people, it should complement your other efforts. Having a virtual bench for a role means that you have options. It means that you have relationships with people that you believe to be A players who would accept an offer for a position with your company.

The goal from both your virtual bench and other recruiting efforts is to end up with five, fully qualified A player candidates who you interview which you then filter down to between two and three who you are genuinely struggling to decide on because they are simply so good. In order to do this you must first cast a wide net, use a variety of sources to have around fifty qualified candidates apply - of course with five candidates being ten percent of fifty. Now I know what you might be thinking, 'we struggle to get a dozen or so qualified candidates to apply for each role at our business, let alone five A players' – well that only identifies the two areas for improvement here: first, to find more talent pools via marketing and other different approaches, and second, to build your virtual bench.

Once you have the fifty applicants, filter them down to around ten whom you conduct telephone interviews with. During these telephone interviews, ask each candidate what Brad Smart refers to as the TORC method or Threat Of Reference Check. This is the truth serum that quickly identifies what type of person you might be talking with, an A player or non-A player. During the telephone interview simply walk back over the past five to seven years of the candidates job history and ask "In that role who did you report to and how will they rate your performance out of ten when we talk with them?". Now remember, most of these direct reports were not offered as references by the candidate.

For an A player, this will be easy, they have left behind a trail of success where people both enjoyed the time working with the former employee and can probably recall specific successful projects they worked on. For non A players, there is probably a lot less consistency, and very quickly you will probably notice that the candidate will be reluctant to share details on every manager they directly reported to in previous years. Remember that the best likelihood that a candidate will be successful in your business is that they have left a trail of success and are probably proud to share!

Story

Anthony ran one of the most successful businesses in the new home building industry and was a firm believer that he was only as good as the people on his team. He knew it was his job to assemble the best team and to help them to achieve great results. A lot of this success came from the sales team, a group of very high performing individuals he had assembled over many years.

When I met with Anthony, he took great pride in showing me his collection of literally hundreds of business cards from sales people within his industry. He believed he had met with almost every person selling new homes in the state, and many outside the state!

He didn't just meet them. The ones he suspected could be superstars on his team, he fostered relationships with, calling or meeting them for coffee each quarter, some over many years, knowing that there wasn't a job available at the time, but one day this person could fill a role on his team. He consistently built these relationships every quarter to become the genuine, viable alternative to their current situation for these salespeople. If ever they were unhappy in their role, or annoyed with their boss, he was the person they called. If Anthony had a vacancy, he would call them and ask if they wanted to apply.

This meant of course that when Anthony had a vacant role, he didn't need to advertise as his virtual bench was so strong that he not only knew everyone who was available and might apply for a job, he knew the superstars who were not available, perhaps a little dissatisfied, and he had a pre-existing relationship with them.

Anthony knew that the best talent didn't apply for jobs but simply went from one role to another because they were in demand.

Tool

The goal here is to have a virtual bench for each significant role with at least two people you are contacting quarterly.

But the first step to achieving that goal is to identify what are the significant roles you need for a virtual bench. For Anthony it was salespeople, designers and construction managers. For a mid-sized business, ask yourself what are the top three roles that could really make a difference to the delivery of your product or service? If you had people who were in the top ten percent of available candidates at the pay rate you provide, in which three roles would these A players have the most impact in your business?

Perhaps after time you can build virtual benches for more than three roles, but three makes a good start.

Once you have identified these three roles, develop an idea for the expected numbers an A player would produce, for Anthony it was salespeople who sold an average of more than three homes per month over a 12 month period.

Then begin to connect with and meet potential candidates. This doesn't need to be a job offer, and it doesn't need to be a commitment for a job offer. But it does need to be flattering to use their ego and the lure of an opportunity to get you a meeting.

Your conversation could simply be; 'Hi it's Brad Giles from Evolution Partners here, I have been given your name by a mutual supplier. In fact I have heard your name mentioned several times recently and I've heard about the great work you have been doing. We're trying as hard as we can to build a great company here and we don't currently have a job available as a sales person, but because I heard your name mentioned I thought I would reach out and see if you would be interested to grab a coffee with me sometime, in case someday we do have a job that you might be interested in?'.

Then meet the person to determine if they might be a potential A player. If they might be, meet them again and again.

For most employees it would be difficult to refuse a simple, broad offer like that with little commitment but a potential opportunity. Then, in the meeting, your primary goal should be to plant a seed in the person's mind that you are a viable alternative to their current job. That's it, obviously you're qualifying them for your role, but also you are positioning yourself as the viable alternative, so that if ever they have a problem, or get fed up with their current job, you are the first person they call.

Once you have a vacancy you can simply say, 'Hi it's Brad from Evolution Partners here, I wanted to let you know that we currently have a vacancy and would love you to apply for the role'. With this approach there is no commitment that they have the job, and it is clear that they will be competing against other candidates, but they should be sufficiently interested from your previous meetings to put in a good effort.

The first step in the table below is to identify the top three impact roles in your business as mentioned above, the roles which will create a meaningful difference if you hired great people in the role. Once you have decided that, next find two people who currently don't work for you, but could work for you, and are possibly in the top 10% of available candidates at the pay you provide. This isn't easy, and you may need to talk to customers, suppliers and industry organisations to find these rare people.

Once you have determined the two bench members for each role, consider what is your next step for each role. It could be a coffee meeting or a phone call or a reference check. But maintain a next step for each role at all times.

Virtual Bench top 3 impact roles

	BENCH MEMBER 1 NAME	BENCH MEMBER 2 NAME	NEXT STEP
Impact role #1			
Impact role #2			
Impact role #3			

 Set yourself simple targets, perhaps one new meeting per week, and begin building your virtual bench.

Key points

★ Great leaders are aware that recruitment is a process that takes time and they are the custodians of the culture.

★ It is beneficial to take more time when hiring to ensure you have the right people.

★ When recruiting, it is beneficial to have pre-existing relationships with potential employees who are in the top 10% of candidates at the pay rate you offer.

Key Resources

★ *Good to Great: Why Some Companies Make the Leap...and Others Don't* - Jim Collins

★ *Topgrading: How Leading Companies Win by Hiring, Coaching and Keeping the Best People* - Brad Smart

5.2 Products and services at risk of decline or disruption are mapped quarterly and actions identified to replace these revenues

Principle

What is the beginning of the end of growth for one of your revenue streams? Is it the day revenues decline or long before this? Once growth has slowed when is it too late?

In his book *The Curve Ahead: Discovering the Path to Unlimited Growth,* Dave Power explains how every revenue stream has a predictable S curve (being low growth followed by high growth and then followed by low growth) and that by analysing each of your revenue streams you are able to determine when growth is slowing and understand when you should work on new strategies and innovations to stimulate growth. Dave suggests that it is possible to 'piggyback' S curves onto each other in order to maintain overall growth by building an innovation process.

More than new ideas or an innovation process, it is important to build a simple process to track growth rates of different revenue streams, to embed a habit within the leadership team of regularly analysing these and an outcome of knowing when to take action to stimulate growth.

Story

David Palmer and Simone Sanders own and operate Miami Bakehouse, one of the most famous bakeries in my state. They have a central bakehouse and a string of retail outlets to sell pies and cakes. Now I knew they were award-winning, but I was pretty impressed when Simone recently told me they had won over 800 awards at baking shows!

While they had established themselves as an award-winning bakery, they didn't have a simple process to map the profit of each item and growth in each item.

Once we mapped the gross profit dollars per week from each product and how it was tracking, we were able to see which products to drop, which to keep, and which to promote during our quarterly offsite sessions. Of course, this had an immediate impact on profitability and the productivity of workers (as the workers were producing more gross profit dollars for their time), which afforded us to fund the next step, when we built a system where an innovation team of four people would meet each month and review new products to go to store. The new products team discussed food trends, what they had seen in the market in magazines and on TV shows, and developed a list of new products that could make it to store. They then filtered the list down to a handful of potential products for the bakery team to work on in the coming month.

Between the monthly meetings the bakery would create the recipes for the new products, knowing that they could not produce products lower than the average gross profit percentage.

Then, at the following monthly meeting for the innovation team, the group would taste test new products. The best four would make it to store for a one-week rotation the following month. This way every week there was a new product of the week, drawing customers to come back to see what the next new product was, thereby increasing average visits.

Of course the best selling products would eventually make it onto the permanent menu to replace the lowest performer.

This then evolved into the three part Brand Promise for the business. Unique flavours, An interesting new flavour each week and Local fresh ingredients daily.

We had built a system to analyse the performance of each revenue stream and to replace the poor performers with new and exciting revenue streams every month, and it worked beautifully.

Tool

How you approach this really depends on the size of your business and the industry you are in. The innovation process we built in the bakery certainly wouldn't work with many of my other clients, but my approach is to understand what best practice in any area is, and then raise the question with the leadership team how they can make this best practice work best in their business. This is my encouragement for you, not to replicate the best practices of others, but to pursue healthy debate around the central question how can you make best practices work best in your business?

Once you have an embedded meeting rhythm which includes the discipline of taking your leadership team offsite every quarter to undertake strategic thinking and execution planning as outlined in chapter 4, build an agenda item for every quarterly offsite meeting to analyse each revenue stream as part of your strategic thinking.

Dedicate time to have each team member understand the revenue growth and gross profit dollars that each revenue stream contributes to the overall performance. Together create a list of priorities that must be executed within the following quarter to improve or cut low performers.

Again, depending on the size of your business, this might only take one hour per quarter either preparing for, or during the quarterly planning session, but the habit of developing this, and the consistent improvement, is what is most important. Another option might be to have the table below partially completed – say the first 6 columns – by the finance department before the quarterly workshop, then provide the form with relevant data and have the leadership team members complete their ideas for the action required column, and come prepared to discuss the action they think is required at the workshop.

In the table below, the first column lists the revenue stream. For example, for the bakery this could be steak and mushroom pies, or all pies, or all baked savoury goods. It depends on how detailed you want to be. In the next column list the revenue dollars for that stream, followed by the gross profit dollars for that stream. In the gross profit margin column, list the percentage of gross profit dollars to revenue.

Product and service gross profit assessment

REVENUE STREAM	REVENUE DOLLARS	GROSS PROFIT DOLLARS	GROSS PROFIT MARGIN	REVENUE STREAM GROSS PROFIT AS A PERCENTAGE OF TOTAL BUSI- NESS GROSS PROFIT DOLLARS	GROSS PROFIT DOLLARS TREND FOR QUARTER AND YEAR FOR THIS STREAM	ACTION REQUIRED
e.g. Stream A, Pipe products	$1,000,000	$375,900	37.59%	52%	8% down Qtr, 12% down year	Launch replacement product

In the following column, compare the gross profit from that stream to all gross profit, and list it as a percentage.

In the sixth column list what is trending within this streams gross profit for the past quarter and the past year. Answer how has the gross profit dollars changed over these two periods. Finally, what action is required based upon this data.

Key points

★ Products and services can gradually decline over time with-out notice.

★ Regular analysis and discussion about profit movements within streams can identify early decline or disruption.

Key Resources

★ *The Curve Ahead: Discovering the Path to Unlimited Growth*
  - Dave Power

5.3 Suppliers at risk of decline or disruption are mapped quarterly and actions identified to replace these suppliers

Principle

Almost every business relies on other businesses to deliver its product or service to customers.

Perhaps it's supplies, materials, systems or sub contractors. Or maybe a cloud computing platform or a software product.

Whatever your business, you rely on people who are employed in other businesses to deliver to you, and you have less certainty over what they will deliver, compared to the certainty you can achieve in your own business. And when you fail to deliver to your customers, they don't care if it was your team, or a vendor or a sub-contractor. You promised to do something, and you failed to deliver. Their trust in you has been broken, and in business trust is everything.

Perhaps you are thinking that you are too large to be concerned by this. Maybe you are relying on multinational companies who have mature systems and platforms that you don't believe will let you down. Well to think that these larger companies aren't affected by quality issues that could impact you is perhaps to readily invite risk into your business. Just consider Samsung, the world's largest mobile phone maker who in 2017 were forced to recall 2.5 million Galaxy Note 7 Smartphones because they randomly caught fire. In fact, there were two recalls around fires. The first stemmed from a design failure in the battery, and the second involved a manufacturing defect that caused more phones to catch on fire. Or perhaps consider Takata, the airbag manufacturer used by virtually every automaker on the planet who produced a faulty airbag inflator that could explode and eject a shrapnel-like material that has been linked to at least 20 deaths and a global recall of more than 100 million inflators, costing over $24 billion.

That's not to mention the countless data breaches, hacks and stolen data that we have all heard about, along with those we haven't heard about.

If you are seeking to achieve consistent growth and consistent results, you must have suppliers who can deliver consistently.

Story

Fiona operates a successful chain of retail stores and is the leading stockist of a particular well known fashion brand. In fact this brand accounted for over 70% of Fiona's revenues year after year and over many years she grew the company adding more and more stores as popularity grew. A few times over the years the factory ran low on one or two items, yet this didn't concern Fiona as she would just order other items that were in stock.

Without her noticing, the global popularity of the product was taking its toll on the factory. The orders were mounting, and the factory was unable to keep up. A few years ago as she was approaching the busy summer period she received a devastating email from her distributor that they weren't going to take on any new orders for four months, and that the factory was only going to deliver the orders it already had in its system.

The decision was timed to suit their winter, when it would have the least impact on retailers in the northern hemisphere, but for Fiona who was heading into an Australian summer, she was going into the busiest period of the year, and unable to receive any shipments from the supplier who provided over 70% of her stock.

All she had was the stock in her warehouse which would be sold in around eight weeks.

As hard as she tried, Fiona was unable to secure new product from either the factory or other retailers. She then knew she was going to lose a lot of money during the time of year she was supposed to make money, the summer.

It was a long, difficult summer for Fiona. While she did lose money, she survived and learnt a great lesson.

Today Fiona has reduced the proportion of product from this supplier from around 70% to 30%, having introduced a number of new brands, all at a higher gross profit margin. Most importantly, Fiona communicates regularly with factories to understand their output capacity and prevent stock outs occurring again.

Fiona has diversified her suppliers to reduce risk and regularly assesses their capability to meet her needs.

Tool

Who are the suppliers you depend upon that could have a material impact on your business?

For example, an office supplies company is unlikely to have a material impact on your business as you would simply get the office stationary from another supplier. However, if your external IT provider creates a problem it may have a material impact on your business. Equally important, if you rely on a sub contractor to deliver and install your product on site, there may be a risk that needs to be monitored.

First, consider all suppliers providing services, product or materials, perhaps even funding. If necessary look through your profit and loss or accounts payable. Next, make a list of all suppliers who could pose a risk of material impact if something went wrong.

If this supplier did create a problem, what would be the impact on a scale of 1 to 10? Place this in the second column. For example, an IT provider could lose all your data, or have your email not working for weeks. Therefore, they would be closer to a 10, whereas a company that prints brochures for you could be very low impact.

Then ask your leaders the question about each supplier 'are there any known threats to be concerned about?' This is not meant to be an exhaustive exercise, simply a regular review of suppliers from a risk perspective.

Finally, given the potential impact and any known threat, what is the action that we need to take?

The IT company mentioned above may be a 10 on the potential impact to the business, yet have no known threats. However, you may not understand the systems they employ to ensure your email stays up and your data isn't lost or hacked.

The action to be taken may be a review to understand that they are in fact adhering to best practice or that your dealing with them is low risk. Then if any suppliers do pose an unacceptable risk, they should be replaced with suppliers who meet your risk requirements.

Supplier risk assessment

SUPPLIERS WHO COULD POSE A MATERIAL RISK	POTENTIAL IMPACT TO THE BUSINESS 1 = LOW 10 = HIGH	ANY KNOWN THREATS TO BE CONCERNED ABOUT	ACTION TO BE TAKEN

Key points

★ Every business relies on other businesses and other people.

★ Suppliers and subcontractors can fail to deliver and cause significant damage to your business.

★ A regular discussion and review can reduce the risk to your consistency.

Key Resources

★ https://en.wikipedia.org/wiki/Samsung_Galaxy_Note_7

★ https://en.wikipedia.org/wiki/Takata_Corporation#Airbag

5.4 All decisions on new opportunities, new staff or new investments are evaluated against a documented set of criteria

Principle

How do you make decisions to invest within your organisation?

In a U.S. survey of 950 CEOs, the National Bureau of Economic Research found that 71 percent of investment decisions are made based upon the reputation of division managers, and further that approximately half of CEOs made decisions based upon gut feel. Sure, gut feel draws upon a person's experience, instincts and training to determine the right decision, yet we know that gut decisions are not necessarily the right decisions.

In his 2017 TED Talk 'Your brain hallucinates your conscious reality' neuroscientist Anil Seth explains how what we observe in the world around us is in fact not reality, but our interpretation of reality, and further that we make decisions based upon a hallucination created by our brain. This hallucination, or our version of reality, is created by the thousands of inputs provided by our five senses at any moment that are then filtered by a process called sensory gating, which in turn helps us to focus on one area of input. For example, if you are crossing the road, you are focussed on the sight and sounds of cars approaching and not the person walking a dog, the music from a café nearby or the sound of the city in the background. These things are still happening around us, but we just don't notice them, and aren't aware of them.

The problem, therefore, is that if we accept that we create our own version of reality based upon these large numbers of sensory inputs over time, the truth is our version of reality, and therefore our perception of reality or a situation, may not be entirely accurate because these thousands of sensory inputs could be affected by any number of external factors such as emotions, medications, sleep deprivation, fitness, hunger, bias or external pressures.

As Margaret Heffernen author of *Willful Blindness: Why We Ignore the Obvious at Our Peril* explains on the subject of critical thinking during tiredness;

'During extreme tiredness glucose is shifted away from critical parts of the brain because the brain wants to stay awake. People can't think critically when tired, and the data tells us that one nights sleep loss is actually worse than being drunk as an impact on critical thinking.'

Should we really rely on CEOs or managers to make gut decisions if they are going through a divorce (emotions), or recovering from an injury (medication), have had a few bad nights sleep (tired), or even are simply under pressure to grow the business unit when these could have a material impact on the quality of the decisions?

Almost worse than making the wrong decisions are the decisions or opportunities that sit there, sucking your mental energy in what I call entrepreneurial white space, a place that your ego loves and yet rarely makes logical sense. Perhaps you run a marketing company and you want to start working in big data, yet don't have core competencies to succeed. So the desire sits there, fed by your ego over months and months, not a yes and not a no. The distraction of entrepreneurial white space fed by the creativity of entrepreneurs who are bored of being managers is one of the largest challenges entrepreneurial leaders must acknowledge and fight against. The best defense: to maintain a disciplined decision-making process to minimise the distraction.

Therefore we can't reliably depend upon 'gut feel' as a decision making tool for critical decisions, as half the CEOs in the survey above mentioned. Instead, a successful CEO needs a simple decision-making criteria to implement across the leadership team to help leaders focus on making the right decisions and importantly to say no to costly distractions and entrepreneurial white space.

Story
In the early 1980s, Ray Dahlio, founder of Bridgewater Capital and

author of the book *Principles: Life and Work* almost lost everything. He had to fire all his staff and was forced to borrow $4,000 from his father to pay household bills. This major event forced him to stop relying on experience, instincts and training (gut) to make decisions. As he puts it 'rather than thinking "I'm right," I started to ask myself, "How do I know I'm right?"'. Ray's newfound humility and self awareness helped him to understand that he could not rely on himself or his managers to consistently make the best decisions and that in fact the only completely reliable method was one known as 'first principles', first taught by Aristotle, whereby only facts and truths are relied on to build an understanding of any subject.

This led Ray to develop approximately two hundred 'principles' to guide the critical decision making process and ensure that the external factors such as bias, medication or sleep deprivation etc mentioned above did not impact the quality of decisions.

Ray developed a set of criteria based upon facts that were known and proven to help his team quickly evaluate opportunities and investment decisions.

According to Ray, these principles are one of the key things that helped him build Bridgewater to have $150 Billion under management in 2016.

Tool

You may not need the 200 criteria that Ray uses; however, for mid market firms, I find that starting with around eight key decision criteria for the CEO and managers to stick to can make a great difference. What we are really trying to do here is two things, first to develop a rigorous investment decision making process and second to develop a system where investment opportunities compete for resources and capital, and the best ideas win. Or as Ray explains, an idea meritocracy, where the best ideas rise to the top from anywhere in the organisation.

Below is an example of a simple funding criteria a client I work with has developed:

Payback period <5 years

Feeds or protects the hedgehog

Net Present Value completed

dLER >$4 for people

Core Capital Target > 2 months

Debt Equity ratio <65%

mLER >$2.50

For a quick definition of terms you may not be familiar with above dLER (Direct Labor Efficiency Ratio) and mLER (Management Labor Efficiency Ratio) are a measure of productivity. dLER measures the dollars returned for every dollar paid to employees who work directly for clients. mLER measures the dollars returned for every dollar paid to management and administration staff.

Core Capital Target is achieved when a business has more than two months of fixed expenses as cash in a separate bank account for no other purpose than to strengthen the business. This provides more liquidity for the business and thereby more strength and strategic options. For more information on LER or Core Capital Target, see Greg Crabtree's book *Simple Numbers, Straight Talk, Big Profits!: 4 Keys to Unlock Your Business Potential*.

We've talked about The Hedgehog already, which comes from Jim Collins' book *Good to Great* and is the strategic discipline achieved by relentlessly maintaining a focus on Core Purpose, Brand Promise and Profit per X.

This simple list of seven items provides a quick go to for anyone who is thinking about seeking an investment within the business and the leadership team agrees to not undertake an investment unless at the very least it meets these criteria.

Once an opportunity has passed this initial criteria it may then need to compete with other opportunities for funding, and I encourage a structured, transparent tool as outlined below.

Here is a simple tool for evaluating opportunities consisting of eight elements.

1. Opportunity and completion
List each of the opportunities, and for each potential investment outline how we know when we have crossed the finish line. For a new sales person they could be making budget. For a new opportunity it could be achieving a profit, for a new investment it could be the time it takes to repay the investment from profits or productivity gains produced.

2. Cost
What will it cost for us to reach the finish line as defined above?

3. Project duration
If we provide the funding, how long will it take to reach the finish line?

4. Recoup from profits
As they like to say on the TV show *Shark Tank,* 'When do I get my money back?' How long will it take us to recoup the invested amount (cost) back from the profits that the opportunity / staff / investment will create?

5. Revenue and profit potential
In five years, if this investment is successful what is likely to be the revenue and profit this investment will produce?

6. Difficulty to complete
Given our core competencies and capabilities how difficult will it be for us to reach the finish line? List a number from very easy 10, to very hard 1.

7. Confidence to complete
How confident are we that we will reach the finish line and generate a profit?

List a number from very easy 10, to very hard 1.

8. Strategic Alignment

How closely does this align with the strategic future we are working to build?

List a number from very closely 10, to not closely 1.

Then tally up the total of the previous three rankings being difficulty, confidence and strategic alignment and enter into total in column 9.

Finally, determine which of the opportunities is more or less important by assessing all opportunities against one another and providing an overall rank as demonstrated below.

The method for this client may not entirely align with the way you prioritise investments; however, the principle remains. Create a simple set of six to ten funding criteria for all leadership team members (including you) to simply assess opportunities and investment decisions. Then treat business investment as a meritocracy where the best investments are the ones which are funded in a competitive and transparent manner.

Finally, when you experience the entrepreneurial white space, indulge the idea, but if it isn't going to meet your funding criteria forget about it as quickly as possible.

Opportunity evaluation sample

1. OPPORTUNITY AND COMPLETION	2. COST	3. PROJECT DURATION	4. RECOUP FROM PROFIT	5. REVENUE PROFIT POTENTIAL	6. DIFFICULTY TO COMPLETE EASY - 10, HARD -1	7. CONFIDENCE TO COMPLETE EASY - 10, HARD -1	8. STRATEGIC ALIGNMENT CLOSELY - 10, NOT CLOSELY -1	9. TOTAL OF THE THREE RANKINGS	OVERALL RANK
A. R&D ON NEW PRODUCT - PROFIT / GOVT GRANT / CLIENT JV	$1m	1 year	10 years	$300k	2	2	6	10	5
B. LAUNCH NEW SERVICE WITH A PROFITABLE CLIENT PROJECT	$250k	1 year	3 years	$200k	5	4	8	17	4
C. SOLAR PANEL INSTALLATION ON OUR ROOF - INSTALLATION COMPLETE	$2m	0.5 year	4 years	$500k cost reduction pa	10	10	2	22	2
D. MARKETING INVESTMENT - 12 NEW CLIENTS	$50k	0.5 year	1 year	$1m	6	6	8	20	3
E. INVEST IN OVERSEAS PARTNERS - 6 NEW COUNTRIES	$200k	0.5 year	1 year	$1m	8	9	10	27	1

Opportunity evaluation tool

1. OPPORTUNITY AND COMPLETION	2. COST	3. PROJECT DURATION	4. RECOUP FROM PROFIT	5. REVENUE PROFIT POTENTIAL	6. DIFFICULTY TO COMPLETE EASY - 10, HARD - 1	7. CONFIDENCE TO COMPLETE EASY - 10, HARD - 1	8. STRATEGIC ALIGNMENT CLOSELY - 10, NOT CLOSELY - 1	9. TOTAL OF THE THREE RANKINGS	OVERALL RANK
A.									
B.									
C.									
D.									
E.									

Key points

★ Decision making is most often done based upon gut instinct.

★ The science demonstrates that our cognitive ability can be significantly affected by emotions, medication, tiredness or stress.

★ It's important to apply a decision making criteria, based upon known facts, to ensure the best decisions are being made consistently.

Key Resources

★ NBER Survey - http://www.nber.org/digest/jan12/w17370.html

★ "Your brain hallucinates your conscious reality" - TED talks - Anil Seth

★ *Willful Blindness - Why We Ignore the Obvious at Our Peril* - Margaret Heffernen

★ *Principles: Life and Work* - Ray Dahlio

★ *Simple Numbers, Straight Talk, Big Profits!: 4 Keys to Unlock Your Business Potential* - Greg Crabtree

5.5 Each leader in the business has appointed a clear successor who could replace them from within

Principle

If leaders in a business are efficient and effective, the momentum of the business builds.

When leaders are skilled and experienced at their job, the momentum of the business builds.

If leaders have the right tools and the right people, the momentum of the business builds.

When a leader in any part of the business leaves, the momentum of the business often decelerates.

The impact of the loss is much greater than most people believe, though, and can be many times the person's salary once you consider:

★ Lost productivity before departure, after departure and after commencement until the person is fully productive

★ Lowered morale and relationship damage to staff and customers

★ Recruiting costs

★ New training and on-boarding costs

The kicker is the 200+ hours wasted by the team each time a person is replaced.

In his research for the book *Topgrading: How Leading Companies Win by Hiring, Coaching and Keeping the Best People*, author Brad Smart found that the typical cost for mis-hiring a manager was 15 times the person's base salary.

Through the work on improving retention in chapter 2 Ambassador and chapter 3 Culture within this book, you should be able to improve your retention rates. However, even if you do improve your retention, people will still leave for a variety of reasons.

When you need to achieve consistent results, it's important to remember that losing and having to replace leaders has a much larger impact on your business than you may suspect and it's important to plan and prepare for any changes.

Think of it like an insurance policy to reduce the impact when someone departs.

But when you do have each leader within the business appoint a clear successor from within, it doesn't mean that person should automatically get their managers job if they leave. In fact the successor should not even know they have been nominated.

Sure, they can apply for the job along with other candidates, and perhaps you may even decide to appoint them in an acting role until the permanent position is decided, but most importantly you have an option to reduce the impact when a leader leaves.

The point is that people are not predictable, and anything can happen.

Story

In June 2010 Ken Talbot, one of Australia's richest men, had booked a room at the Yaounde Hilton Hotel, the most luxurious hotel in Cameroon in order to commemorate his company, Sundance Resources, expansion into Africa from Western Australia and for the company's first formal meeting on Cameroon soil.

Sundance were working with local joint venture partner Cam Iron to mine the potentially billion-tonne Mbalam iron ore project in Cameroon's East Region and this important project was a key part of the ambitious African nations goals to unlock its natural resources.

After meeting with the Cameroon Prime Minister and some of the country's most senior businesspeople, Ken and other members of the board had planned a visit to the Mbalam iron ore project. Unfortunately, they were unable to get the required clearances to travel into Congolese airspace in an arranged charter plane as the project was about 10 kilometers inside the Republic of Congo. They had to settle on a Casa C212, a smaller aircraft with an unenviable safety record.

The original plan was to have Ken take his private jet and other members use the original chartered plane when it was subsequently realised that Ken's private jet was too big to land on the remote air strip at Mbalam, so it was decided that one plane would be chartered for the entire board.

Tragically the plane crashed in the Congo jungle 30 kilometres short of Mbalam, and 11 people died in the crash including Ken, the CEO Don Lewis and the entire board of Sundance Resources.

The day after the crash, chief financial officer Peter Canterbury assumed the role of acting chief executive. However, without a succession plan, rebuilding the entire board was an incredibly difficult undertaking.

While this is an extreme example of the need for succession planning and the importance of risk mitigation, every day around the world people in key roles depart for a variety of reasons, significantly impacting the consistency of results produced by their businesses. In the event a person in a key role departs the business your first call shouldn't be to a recruiter, it should be to the person you already know can step into the role with minimal impact.

Tool

First think about who are the leaders in the business that really need to have a potential successor appointed. This doesn't necessarily mean only your leadership team, nor is it extended to all people who manage a team. If a leader wasn't to come to work again from tomorrow onward for whatever reason, if there would be a significant impact on the business, then a successor may be required.

The point here is if that were to happen you could approach the successor and explain to them that they had to stop doing their current job and do the missing leaders role in an acting capacity until the vacancy was filled. This person may not be fully qualified to do the role, and in some circumstances, there may even be a legal or compliance issue, the point is that at the very least having someone to deal with customers, suppliers, staff and everything else that comes along is better than you, or their manager stepping into that role. Of course, the appointed, acting successor will require support and guidance and you should provide that to them in abundance, but they are the one to take ownership of the role, in a temporary manner, until it is filled.

Once you know the roles that require a successor, meet individually with the leaders and discuss who should step up in their absence and why it should be that person. Agree on one person for every role and maintain the list over time.

Leadership succession plan

ROLE	PERSON TO SUCCEED	WHY

Key points

★ A leader departing can significantly impact the growth and results of a business.

★ Being able to rapidly respond when a leader departs can reduce this impact.

★ Having each leader nominate a successor can provide an option to appoint a temporary replacement, thereby ensuring that the leaders work is still being done.

Key Resources

★ *Topgrading: How Leading Companies Win by Hiring, Coaching and Keeping the Best People* - Brad Smart

★ NEXT STEPS

Thank you for reading *Made to Thrive.*

To make your potential count for more, for you to have a greater impact in this world of effort, requires change from where you are today. Whatever your score on the *Made to Thrive* checklist was, it will take effort to improve and achieve greater results. And this change isn't easy.

The human body is made up of multiple systems such as the respiratory system, the nervous system and the endocrine system. Yet above these systems is the process called homeostasis where all organ systems work together to maintain a stable environment. Any minor change, detected via positive or negative feedback, quickly triggers a reaction elsewhere in the body to counteract the change in order to maintain the overall stability of the body.

The equivalent to the overall homeostasis process is also present within organizations when it comes to initiating change. As you begin to initiate the changes described in this book, regardless of whether those changes are determined to be positive or negative by the people in the organization, a reaction will occur to counteract that change, because the overall collective of the organization has a subconscious desire to maintain stability.

You need to appreciate just how hard it is to break your company's homeostasis.

This is why so many change initiatives and strategy initiatives fail in the execution phase. The intent of you and your leaders may be pure. You may be trying to implement change to help the company and help your people to thrive, but to do that you must first overcome the company's homeostasis – all the systems, processes, attitudes and beliefs that already exist.

To give you the best chance to implement the concepts contained within this book successfully, consider these five best practices.

Begin at the beginning

Your first job should be to identify which of the twenty five ideas in this book will have the greatest impact. Implement that one first. Then choose the second, the third and so on. It's one thing to complete a tool within the book, it's another to have it successfully working within your company. Work on one thing at a time from the most impactful to the least impactful.

If you really don't know where to start, start with culture. Focus your energy for a quarter on *Made to Thrive* checklist item 3.1, having all employees in your company know your Core Values and Core Purpose. Focus on it relentlessly until your people mock you for it. Then the next quarter, move onto 3.2 on the checklist and embed a qualitative and quantitative system of feedback between all employees and leaders. Once you can tick all five of the culture boxes on the checklist, move counter-clockwise around the star onto ambassador, beginning with 2.1 and work through that and then onward in a counter-clockwise direction around the star.

Use agendas

The challenge with new initiatives as outlined above is the desire to revert to the way things were. New initiatives need two points of accountability. First, a person who is accountable to report, and second, a time when the accountable person will report. Many of the tools in this book can be built into the permanent agenda of your weekly, monthly or quarterly meeting. By appointing a person to report and allocating time within your agenda, you ensure that these tools will not only become embedded, but will remain into the future.

Use data

When you implement one of these tools, and you have a person accountable, ensure its measured. For example, if you have started with *Made to Thrive* checklist item 3.1, having all employees in your company know your Core Values and Core Purpose and it's your focus for the quarter, measure it through the quarter. Of course, do this in a way that suits the culture of your company, but don't just guess. Make the measurement of progress the key talking point in your agenda meetings during the implementation phase.

Use a coach

Top athletes and sports teams know it's not possible to achieve peak performance without a coach. The right coach for you, for your leadership team, with the right fit and an external perspective will genuinely challenge you to go beyond your comfort zone.

There is no doubt that some coaches are better than others in the business world, as in the sports world. You wouldn't expect a youth soccer coach to be a great coach in the national league with a team of elite athletes.

Just like the sports' world, the elite coaches are in great demand and will cost more, but can have a significant impact on a serious business endeavouring to thrive. You need to be confident that any coach is the right fit for you.

If you need help implementing these tools, I'd be happy to introduce you to some of our certified coaching partners across the globe. You can find me at brad.giles@evolutionpartners.com.au, where I'd love to hear from you.

Enjoy the journey

Even though there is a lot of work to do in this book, work that takes time, the intent is to ultimately give you more time. Time for the sake of usefulness in the world; for the sake of helping those we love; for the sake of benefitting society.

You should have less time stuck in operational matters, and more time to work on the more important and less urgent matters. Because success isn't taking a larger fortune to your grave, it's about enjoying all the signposts along the way.

So smile, laugh, celebrate the wins and inject some enjoyment into your journey.

CPSIA information can be obtained
at www.ICGtesting.com
Printed in the USA
LVHW031426281019
635532LV00006B/844/P